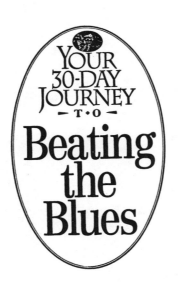

YOUR
30-DAY
JOURNEY
— T·O —
Beating
the
Blues

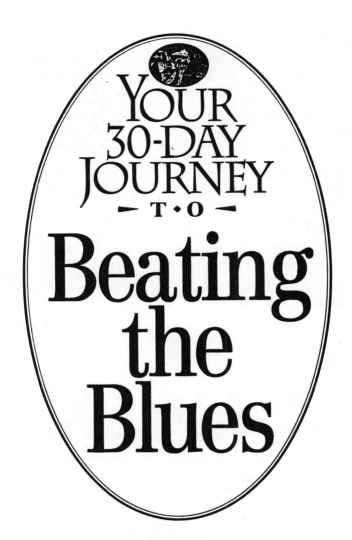

YOUR 30-DAY JOURNEY —T·O—

Beating the Blues

OLIVER NELSON

THOMAS NELSON PUBLISHERS
Nashville

Copyright © 1992 by Stephen Arterburn and Connie Neal

Published in Nashville, Tennessee, by Oliver-Nelson Books, a division of Thomas Nelson, Inc., Publishers, and distributed in Canada by Lawson Falle, Ltd., Cambridge, Ontario.

The Bible version used in this publication is THE NEW KING JAMES VERSION. Copyright © 1979, 1980, 1982, Thomas Nelson, Inc., Publishers.

Scripture quotation noted NRSV is from the New Revised Standard Version of the Bible. Copyright © 1989 by the Division of Christian Education of the National Council of the Churches of Christ in the United States of America.

The individuals described in this book are composites of real persons whose identities are disguised to protect their privacy.

Printed in the United States of America.

Library of Congress Cataloging-in-Publication Data

Neal, C. W. (Connie W.), 1958–
    Your 30-day journey to beating the blues / C.W. Neal.
        p.   cm.
    ISBN 0-8407-9643-9 (pbk.)
    1. Depression, Mental—Popular works. 2. Self-help techniques.
    I. Title. II. Title: Your thirty-day journey to beating the blues.
RC537.N43   1992
616.85'27—dc20   92-24145
                                                                          CIP

1   2   3   4   5   6   —   97   96   95   94   93   92

Contents

Introduction

Self-help programs of any kind require motivation, hope, and clarity of mind to get you moving in a positive direction. When you've got the blues, you probably lack motivation, have lost hope, and find your thoughts confused. Taking any journey requires energy to get you from where you are to where you want to be. When you are depressed, you don't feel like doing much of anything, not even taking a journey that promises relief.

This book is designed with the understanding that if you need to take the journey, you probably don't feel like it, and you may not be able to do some of what needs to be done to beat the blues on your own. When you've got the blues, the tendency is to draw away from people and normal interactions of everyday life. Isolation is a major obstacle to beating the blues because you will need support from someone whose perspective is not clouded to help you see your way clear.

You will take this journey with a friend or loved one who is concerned about you. To whatever degree you are able to take the steps on your own, you are encouraged to do so with that person's support. To whatever degree you need to lean on your support person, he or she is guided to carry the weight you cannot bear until you are able. If someone in your life has said, "I wish I knew how to help you," give the individual this book, and ask for support on your journey.

You may be reading this introduction because you are concerned for a friend or loved one who is depressed. He doesn't seem able or willing to help himself, and you want to help. That is good. She may be debilitated in ways that make it nearly impossible for her to beat the blues without help. If you are looking for a starting place to help the person break free of depression, this book will lead the way. It will also educate you regarding the important role you play in the recovery.

The format of the book is designed for the person who is trying to beat the blues. Each day there will be information, personal evaluation, action, and encouragement. There will also be support notes addressed to the support person, explaining the role and what to do to help the person on the journey.

This book is written on the basis of three beliefs:

1. *There is hope, even if you can't feel hope right now.* You can begin moving in the direction of relief before you feel hopeful. In fact, if you wait until you feel like helping yourself, you will stay mired in depression. The instructions in this journey will be strongly directive. You will be told clearly what steps you need to take and how to take them. You are not expected to feel like taking them or to even have hope that they will help. As you begin taking steps in the direction of health,

you will become able to feel hope at some point along the way.

2. *When you've got the blues, it is difficult to think clearly.* Some symptoms of depression are being unable to concentrate, having clouded thoughts, laboring to keep your mind focused, and feeling overwhelmed by minor decisions that need to be made. These symptoms are experienced intellectually and emotionally but may be caused by physical conditions affecting your brain chemistry. Your thoughts may be slow in getting through or labored because of real biological causes. For this reason, the style of this book will be straightforward and as simple as possible. What you do in response to this book, not the style, is significant in terms of beating the blues.

3. *You sincerely want to resume a normal life, even if you don't act like it.* Many times when you are depressed, you appear unwilling to help yourself, irritable, or uncooperative. Those around you may assume you don't sincerely want to find a way out of your darkened mood. This assumption can provoke harsh judgmental reactions, which do nothing to help anyone in the situation. Therefore, this journey will be guided in a nonjudgmental and compassionate way, accepting that you don't want to be miserable. The instructions given to the support person will educate him or her to see beyond your symptoms and respond with compassion rather than react harshly. However, because you acknowledge your desire to recover and you have a support person to help you do what you are not

able, you will be expected to take each action step without using your symptoms as an excuse for remaining in depression.

Picking up this book shows your need and desire to find relief from living with the blues. This path can lead you back to the level of health that allows you to enjoy life once more. It is my sincere hope that this journey marks a turning point in your life, which will lead you to a brighter future.

Finding a Companion for Your Journey

This is one journey you dare not take alone. You may not want to be in a close relationship with anyone when you've got the blues, or you may fear that no one wants to be around you when you're in such a bad mood, but you will need support in your journey to make the kinds of changes that will allow you to enjoy life again.

The reason it is necessary to have a support person every step of the way is that the symptoms of depression can restrict your ability to think clearly enough to make accurate personal evaluations. Depression can also sap your strength so that you can't do the things necessary to recover. If there is a physiological or biochemical cause, a support person can keep you moving until you have received treatment for any medical problems that contribute to your lack of energy and lowered mood.

Some depression comes from repressed trauma or suppressed emotions, which become a source of shame and fear. The more you keep them to yourself, the more you add to your depression. If you discover clues to this while on your journey, you will need someone to affirm love for you as you decide how to face potentially painful memories. Without your support person's objectivity and encouragement, you might be blind to the clues of this type of origin or purposely avoid the very issues that may be at the root of your depression.

Your companion for this journey does not need to be a counselor; that is not the role required. Your support person is not responsible to fix you. Only you can take responsibility for your life. You need someone by your side who will give you honest feedback, keep you motivated to take the next step, and help you get the assistance you need once you figure out what might be beneficial.

You need to look for these qualifications in your support person: someone . . .

- who will encourage you
- who has a positive outlook on life
- who does not hold a preconceived notion of what you need to do to "snap out of it"
- who will allow you to express honest thoughts and sincere feelings without trying to fix them or negate them
- who knows how to listen
- who will give you honest feedback
- who will keep your confidences
- who has time available
- who will hold you accountable and help you keep your commitment to complete this journey

PERSONAL EVALUATION

Take a moment to think of someone who could act as your support person on this journey. Also decide on a second choice if that person is unavailable. You may want to think of friends, people in a support group, relatives *(only* if they are supportive and can keep your journey confidential), members of your church, synagogue, or other organizations.

ACTION

Contact the person you have in mind to lend you support for the journey, and explain what is involved in the commitment. Let the person read the first two days of this journey before you ask for a decision.

If the person declines to play this role, don't automatically assume that to mean a lack of love. Many people have a hard time watching someone they love struggle emotionally and feel the depths of pain associated with depression without being able to magically make the pain go away.

SUPPORT NOTES

If you are being asked to be of support during this journey, read over the list of qualifications and see if you have what it takes. Remember, you are not being asked to play the role of a counselor or therapist. In fact, you need to refrain from doing so. You are simply being asked to be a faithful friend who will provide support, encouragement, and a clear perspective to help your loved one complete each day's journey.

ENCOURAGEMENT

The first step toward beating the blues is the step out of isolation. Your willingness to reach out for help will be rewarded.

FOOD FOR THOUGHT

Two are better than one, because they have a good reward for their toil. For if they fall, one will lift up the other; but woe to one who is alone and falls and does not have another to help.
—Ecclesiastes 4:9–10 NRSV

Your Commitment to the Journey

Although the symptoms of depression are common, the causes and cures are unique for each individual. Because there are typically several factors working together and crossing the lines between body, mind, and spirit, you need to make sure your evaluation goes far enough to include all contributing factors, then deal with each appropriately. If you jump to conclusions or try to apply what worked for someone else directly to your situation, you may be sadly disappointed. Therefore, you need to commit yourself to completing the entire journey so that you have a complete picture of the problem and a complete solution.

To take this journey, you will need a glimmer of hope, a tiny speck of faith, and a fair amount of courage. All of them will be put into action through your determined commitment to complete this journey. You have demonstrated a glimmer of hope by picking up this book. You also have access to faith and courage, whether you realize it or not.

A simple definition of faith is being willing to do something to reach toward what you hope for in the future. You exercise faith every day. When you reach for the light switch, you are exhibiting faith, doing something you believe will give you the light you need. When you began this journey, you demonstrated that you have at least a little faith, and that is all you need.

Courage is not an absence of fear. Courage is determining to use the strength and resources you have to take steps in the right direction, even though you are afraid. You can find courage within yourself, gain courage from trust in a loving God who will never leave you in the midst of life's battles, and draw courage from others who have been able to overcome depression and from people willing to encourage you. Gather up all the courage within your reach, and determine to commit yourself to complete this journey.

Here is the commitment you are being asked to make:

1. Read the material each day, make the personal evaluation, and take the action steps suggested.
2. Follow the daily routine for basic health (walking, taking a multivitamin, resting, eating nourishing foods).
3. Be honest with yourself and your support person.
4. Accept help from others when you are unable to help yourself.

Your support person will also need to make a commitment to you and your journey. The commitment will include the following:

1. Take time with you each day to go over the personal evaluation, help with the action steps, and provide support needed to supplement what you are able to do for yourself.
2. Give up prejudices about the cause and cure of your depression.
3. Keep your confidences.
4. Persevere through this 30-day journey, even though it may be difficult.

PERSONAL EVALUATION

Are you willing to commit yourself to this journey?

ACTION

My Personal Commitment

I, _____, am willing to invest at least 30 minutes a day, from each of the next 30 days, to focus on this journey. I plan to take this time *(circle one)* each morning, around noon, each afternoon, each evening, or before bedtime.

During this journey, I will do the following to care for my health on a daily basis: go for a twenty-minute walk, take a multivitamin, eat nourishing foods, and give myself enough time to rest.

I am willing to accept support to help me complete each day's personal evaluation and action steps. I am willing to be honest with myself and my support person. I will also consider accepting whatever help I need to deal with the cause of my depression.

I make this commitment to myself this _____ day of _____, 19_____.

_____

Signature

SUPPORT NOTES

If you are willing to begin this journey, you must also be willing and able to commit yourself to see the journey through to the end. You must have the time available to discuss the daily reading and evaluation and also to assist with the action steps required. Depending on the severity of the depression, you may be the one doing most of the work, initially carrying the burdens your loved one can't handle. Sentiment is not enough. You must have patience, energy, encouragement, an open ear, and a loving heart available. If you have these to offer and are willing to see this journey through to the end, you can play a tremendous role in helping your loved one beat the blues.

Here is the commitment you are considering:

Commitment of Support

I, _____, am willing to invest at least 30 minutes a day, from each of the next 30 days, to focus on this journey with you. The time I have available to talk with you and go over the personal evaluation and action steps is: weekdays _____, and weekends _____ _____.

The time I am not available is after _____ each night and before _____ each morning.

I will encourage you to care for your basic health on a daily basis and hold you accountable to complete your daily commitment. I am/am not *(circle one)* available to walk with you each day.

I am willing to support you to the degree you need my help to complete each day's personal evaluation and action steps. I am willing to keep your confidences to myself. I will do the best I can to encourage you to complete this journey. If I feel the help you need is beyond what I can confidently offer, I will try to get you the kind of help you need and remain your friend.

I make this commitment to you this _____ day of _____, 19_____.

_____

Signature

Note: You can add any additional comments you would like to limit or expand your commitment suitable to your particular situation.

Finding Motivation (When You Don't Feel Like Moving)

To keep yourself moving toward any goal, you need to become aware of the benefits you will receive. That is usually as simple as thinking about your goal and imagining what your rewards will be once you reach it. When beating the blues is your goal, it may not be so simple. Your times of reflection may consistently turn toward negative thoughts and remind you of your overwhelming sense of hopelessness. Your support person can help you identify the benefits you will receive from completing this journey.

There are three areas where being relieved of depression will have a dramatic effect: finding relief from the emotional pain, being able to enjoy your life, and improving the lives of your family members. Beating the blues will bring relief from the pain you are suffering. You may find relief from inner pain, gloom, and despair that may not have an identifiable cause. You may find relief from the results of emotional injury that has never been acknowledged or treated, unresolved grief over some loss in your life, or the belief that you are trapped in a hopeless situation. You may find relief from a deep sense of shame and the fear there is something so terribly wrong with you that you would be utterly rejected if you were ever to share the depths of what troubles you at your innermost level. You may also be surprised to find relief from physical pain such as headaches, stomach disturbances, exhaustion, neck and back pain, and other chronic health problems.

Beating the blues will positively affect your life: your inner life, your relationships, and your work. It is obvious that your inner life would be much better if you weren't miserable. But you may not see far enough to realize how dramatically your relationships and work are affected by your mood. Every relationship is limited by your inability to enjoy life. Your love relationships, your friendships (or lack thereof), your relationships with family members who have to cope with how your darkened mood keeps you from fulfilling your role in the family, your work relationships with your boss and those under your authority—virtually all of your relationships are limited and potentially damaged by ongoing depression that is not treated effectively. Consider how much better your life could be if you didn't have to continually swim upstream against the force of your depressed mood.

Beating the blues will allow you to be what your loved ones need you to be. There are people in your life who need you to give of yourself to them. When you are feeling miserable and worthless, you are not going to be contributing fully to personal relationships. The person on the other side of the relationship misses out on something valuable when you are not able to give of yourself. This is especially true if you are a parent. Your children need you to be there to meet their needs. If you are consumed by depression and unable to see beyond the darkness that envelops your life, your children suffer a significant loss. Even if your low self-regard tells you they aren't missing out on anything of significance by your lack of involvement in their lives, they are. Maybe you are aware of this issue and feel tremendous guilt as a part of your suffering. Your love for your children can be a powerful motivating force that keeps you moving toward recovery. Tap into it and use it.

PERSONAL EVALUATION

Consider how you could benefit from beating the blues, overcoming depression, and being able to enjoy life again.

- In what ways do you want to experience relief from the pain?
- What relationships with loved ones could be better if you were not depressed?
- What relationships at work could be improved?
- What could be improved in your view of yourself?
- When you consider the people closest to you, who rely on you to meet needs in their lives, how could you better meet their needs if you weren't depressed?
- When was the last time you were really able to

enjoy a special time in your life, perhaps a holiday or vacation?

ACTION

Write out a list of benefits for your life that will result from beating the blues. You don't have to be able to dream of these things happening to put them on the list. As best you can, discuss the possibilities with your support person, and make a list of what would be better in your life if you were free from depression. Read over them periodically to remind yourself why it is so important to keep moving ahead on your journey. You may also use this list as a basis for prayer, asking God to help you find your way to reach these benefits.

SUPPORT NOTES

You may be able to see clearly how much better life would be for your loved one and be able to envision a hopeful future for him. He may not be able to see that far. It is good to verbalize your hopeful vision for his future as long as you don't insist that he be able to envision it with you. He may be able to see only what is wrong, what is missing, what is upsetting or frustrating. Don't try to make him feel the hope you feel for him at this point. Just help him turn his list of negatives around to be a list of positive reasons to overcome whatever is causing the darkened moods.

For example, if he says, "I hate myself," the item on the list of benefits would be: to be able to accept myself as being valuable. If he says, "I can't function at work; I hate my job, but I'm afraid I'm going to be fired," the item on the list would be: to be able to succeed at work and have greater security in my career.

Once the list of negatives is turned around into positive benefits, read the list to him and encourage him that he can receive these benefits. If both of you feel comfortable praying together, offer to pray for these benefits to be realized in his life.

ENCOURAGEMENT

These benefits are a real possibility for you once you deal with the true source of your depression. Even though you may not believe that you will lay hold of them, your willingness to take this journey will bring them within your reach.

The Path You Follow Will Be Unique

Although depression can be caused in several ways, the symptoms are similar. You feel low. You lose interest or pleasure in what you used to enjoy. You have depressed moods even when your circumstances are good. There is a marked shift in your behavior. You cry easily. You lack motivation —you don't care anymore. You have trouble sleeping, or you sleep all the time. You lose your appetite and lack interest in sex. You are fatigued. You have general thoughts of death or suicide. You are unable to concentrate, and thought processes seem slowed. You feel overwhelmed by simple decisions. You are pessimistic. Your feelings of guilt are intense (whether or not they are legitimate). You struggle with low self-esteem, feeling worthless, unwanted, unloved, dirty, or sinful. You can't function well with others socially and at work. You lose your motivation to care for personal needs such as eating, grooming, personal hygiene, and so on. You are irritable, overreacting to little problems. You are beset by physical discomforts and maybe even chronic pain, which may be quite severe.

Most people have experienced some form of depression. They recall experiencing these kinds of feelings, and they have a theory about what caused them and how they were able to get out of their bout of depression. Their theory about the cause and cure of their bout with the blues will reflect their general focus in life. A medical doctor may focus more on the possible physical factors; a pastor, priest, or other spiritual adviser may focus on the spiritual influences; a counselor or psychologist may focus on the relational or psychological roots of depression; someone who has experienced the power of positive thinking may see depression primarily in terms of having a negative mind-set.

You have probably heard people espousing their beliefs about what you need to do to get over your bout with the blues. Rather than choose to focus on one of these perspectives, you need to develop your own theory that considers all these factors.

You are a whole person: body, mind, and spirit. You have had unique experiences, developed your own beliefs and relationships that will play a part in the puzzle of what needs to be done in your life to beat the blues. Any perspective that focuses on one part of life to the exclusion of others will fall short of revealing the whole picture you need to consider. The causes of your depression are a unique blend of physical, emotional, mental, spiritual, and experiential factors. So the cure will be a unique prescription that is able to deal with whatever is at the source of your condition.

You may find that people often try to prescribe for you what helped them. They are probably well meaning and perhaps convinced that you could beat the blues if you would do what they say.

However, you will frustrate yourself if you expect what worked for someone else to work for you in the same way. You can gain hope from their common experience of feeling as you do now and being able to break free. You can gain insight into possible contributing factors to be considered, but no one else's cure will magically make your pain go away.

PERSONAL EVALUATION

Are you willing to accept that there may be influences in the following areas of life that contribute to your depression?

- Physical/biological conditions   Yes ☐   No ☐
- Emotional/psychological
  conditions   Yes ☐   No ☐
- Spiritual influences   Yes ☐   No ☐
- Mental/intellectual influences   Yes ☐   No ☐
- Relational or experiential
  influences   Yes ☐   No ☐

Are there people in your life who tell you that you could overcome your depression if you would just do what they say? Who are they? What are their theories about the causes and cure of your depression? Can you see how their focus in life influences their perspective on what would help you beat the blues?

ACTION

You are going to consider the input of the people who care enough about you to have offered their theory on what could help you. Individually, these ideas may be lacking; however, when taken together, the feedback from people who care for you and observe you can be a helpful source of information as you develop and test your own theories about the causes and cure for your condition.

Across the top of a sheet of paper, list the following: "Who?"; "The Theory"; "The Advice"; "Primary Focus." In the column under each heading, list the name of anyone who has cared enough to comment on your depression, the theory about what the cause might be, and the advice. Under "Primary Focus," note if the person tends to see things primarily from one perspective: physical, psychological, spiritual, intellectual, or relational.

After each one, write yes, no, or maybe to state whether you believe the perspective may be a valid part of the causes and cure of your condition.

SUPPORT NOTES

You may have your own theories that can be a helpful part of understanding the unique factors contributing to your friend's depression. You can include them in the discussion; however, please don't try to persuade her to accept your perspective. Your job is to help her gather as complete a picture as possible. Your objectivity is what is needed at this point.

During this phase, it is more important to ask questions to help her uncover what might be important pieces of the puzzle rather than to tell her what you think. Remember, she has more access to the answers for the problem than you do.

ENCOURAGEMENT

Your willingness to broaden your perspective will give you a clearer picture of the factors contributing to your condition. Once your focus is clearer, your journey to finding real solutions will be easier to follow.

Dealing with Your Addictions

You cannot overcome depression while relying on addictive-compulsive behavior to alter your mood, especially if you are using drugs and/or alcohol, which are depressants. Depression and addictions feed on one another. If you are in bondage to some form of addiction, it will have a dramatic impact on your ability to identify the source of your depression. You need to deal with your addictive-compulsive behavior simultaneously when you deal with your depression.

Sometimes emotional pain can be a helpful indicator of problems needing attention and care. Just as a doctor might use indications of pain to diagnose a problem and guide you in selecting a treatment, your experience of pain can help you identify issues that may contribute to your depression. Facing this pain can be the first step in finding the kind of help you need to heal whatever emotional injuries you may have.

Any addiction involves using a mood-altering substance or experience to temporarily escape the pain of life. If you deaden the pain with an addiction, you distract yourself momentarily, but you do nothing to identify and deal with the source of your pain. When you use an addiction to mask the pain, you lose touch with your sense of what is really hurting and what needs attention. In this way your use of an addiction can keep you in depression because it covers the real source of your pain.

An addiction will make you feel better for a while, but once the emotional high is gone, you need progressively more of whatever it is you use to get the previous level of relief. Eventually, you may violate your values in hopes of deadening the pain. You then have to cope with guilt, self-condemnation, and the consequences of your behavior, which can be depressing! Trying to medicate the pain of the moment can lead to physical dependency on alcohol and drugs, which also adds to your ongoing depression.

Addictive-compulsive behavior will drag you back into depression, and depression can draw you back into addictive-compulsive behavior. It is a vicious cycle that must be stopped at the point of the addiction while also dealing with the depression.

Breaking through denial and admitting that you have an addiction are monumental steps forward in overcoming depression. You may experience a tremendous amount of fear and hesitation at the thought of having to give up what has been your only source of relief. This reaction is completely understandable, but you must overcome this hesitation to get well again. If you decide to deal with your addiction and depression simultaneously, you may find a way to be free of your need for the addiction. If you refuse to consider that you are in bondage to an addiction, you are seriously limiting your ability to find lasting freedom from depression.

PERSONAL EVALUATION

You may not feel comfortable telling your support person the exact nature of your addictive-compulsive behavior. You don't have to. What is important is that you acknowledge addictive-compulsive behavior and decide to get appropriate help.

What do you do to temporarily alter your mood when you are feeling pain associated with depression?

What substances or experiences do you use to escape the pain of living your life? Place a check next to any addictions you have used at any time in the past. Check any of these addictive-compulsive behaviors you currently use (within the last six months).

- ☐ Alcohol
- ☐ Marijuana
- ☐ Narcotics
- ☐ Sex addiction (including the use of pornography or any form of sexual stimulation)
- ☐ Relational/romance addiction
- ☐ Compulsive gambling
- ☐ Compulsive overeating
- ☐ Compulsive spending

- ☐ Codependency (losing yourself in the needs of others)
- ☐ Workaholism
- ☐ Religious addiction
- ☐ Other: _____

ACTION

If you are overwhelmed by the thought of trying to face life without your addiction to help you cope, consider whether an inpatient treatment program would enable you to break the cycle. Call an inpatient treatment program, and talk to a staff person about the program and how it might work for you. (There is no obligation, and the call can be anonymous.)

Do something today to seek treatment for your addictive or compulsive behavior. Call a treatment program; attend a support group or a twelve-step group; tell your support person that you realize you may have an addiction to deal with; make an appointment with a counselor who specializes in helping those with your particular addiction.

SUPPORT NOTES

If the person is willing to acknowledge addictive-compulsive behavior, help him take the steps necessary to get on the road to recovery. Denial is a powerful deterrent. If you see there is a problem with addiction that he is ignoring, speak honestly about what you see. If he feels uncomfortable reaching out for help but is willing to receive it, you make the calls and arrange for him to speak with someone in an appropriate treatment program. It may take time to research and locate treatment that fits with his values, schedule, and financial considerations. His willingness to accept treatment is a major effort on his part. Your part is to make the practical arrangements to get him into the treatment program he needs.

ENCOURAGEMENT

Living without your addiction does not have to mean a life of ongoing pain and depression. You have the best chance possible of finding a way to enjoy life by dealing with your depression while also seeking treatment for your addictions.

The Progression Out of the Pit

Having the blues can result from something as simple as becoming depleted emotionally, physically, or spiritually. Your journey will be progressive so that if your bout with the blues is a matter of exhaustion in some area of life, you can remedy the simple problem with a simple solution. You will start with actions aimed at nourishing yourself in basic ways and move on to look further if basic nourishment and self-care don't resolve your problem.

You will start by making simple changes, ensuring that your basic needs are being met. If your bout of the blues is related to something simple, it may clear up by taking care of yourself—body, mind, and spirit—and nurturing primary relationships. If your depression is related to something more than a depletion of a basic need, you will be able to recognize that when the condition isn't resolved by nourishing yourself. You may also realize the severity of the problem when you try to practice basic self-care and find yourself unable to do so. If you do need to look deeper, the improvements in your general health will give you added strength to continue your journey until you can identify and resolve the source of your depression.

Starting today, you will do the following to improve your basic health:

- Take a multivitamin/mineral supplement.
- Eat nourishing foods from the recommended food groups during your meals. You may also want to use a diet supplement or healthful drink to give you the nourishment your body needs if your depression has caused you to lose your appetite. If you don't have someone to fix your meals and you lack the energy to prepare nutritious meals, take advantage of readily available healthy meals that require minimal preparation (salad bars, healthy frozen meals, etc.).
- Take a daily walk of at least twenty minutes. It is best done outside in the sunshine if weather permits. If weather or scheduling doesn't allow you to walk outdoors during daylight hours, find another alternative. Consider walking inside a shopping mall or other enclosed building. You may want to take your walk with your support person and use the time to discuss your journey for the day.
- Get enough rest. Arrange your schedule to allow sufficient sleep each night. When you sleep, your body has the opportunity to replenish certain brain chemicals that help you function normally. Whenever you are not getting enough sleep, particularly deep sleep, you are more likely to experience irritability, mood swings, and depressed feelings.

You may find that you are troubled by a sleep

disturbance, either being unable to sleep or sleeping excessively, which is a common symptom of depression. Try your best to get adequate rest. If you cannot sleep, do something restful such as reading, and allow your body to rest even though sleep escapes you. Beware of becoming dependent on sleep-inducing medication or narcotics. Also cutting back on caffeine can promote better rest for your body.

PERSONAL EVALUATION

- Are you willing to make these basic changes in your daily life?
- Will you need help from your support person to change your schedule, eating habits, and daily routine?
- What practical obstacles seem to be in your way that would need to be overcome to begin basic self-care today?

ACTION

Check to see if you have a good multivitamin/mineral supplement. If you don't, get a bottle today. You can call your local health food store and ask for recommendations.

Ask your support person to help you plan your meals so that you are sure to be eating a nutritious, balanced diet.

Take your walk today, and plan the time each

day you will take your walk for the remainder of your journey.

Go to bed early tonight.

SUPPORT NOTES

Making any kind of change from a normal routine takes practice, even when you are not depressed. For the person who is depressed, these simple changes may seem overwhelming. You may need to take charge and provide these changes for your loved one. If you can, take the walk with her. You may even need to get her up and going. Use the time to talk about the day's journey. Be patient with her feelings but insistent that she take these steps that will help her.

Encourage her to tell you any obstacles she sees that would keep her from making these changes. Then take it upon yourself to eliminate the obstacles for her.

ENCOURAGEMENT

When you do these basic things to care for yourself, you are giving yourself the best foundation for being able to beat the blues.

Taking Care of Your Physical Health

Depression is experienced as an emotional condition, but it is often related to physical conditions, routines, and behaviors. By taking care of your body, inside and out, you can remedy any health conditions that cause or contribute to depression.

You can best help yourself beat the blues by making sure you are in good physical health. Depression can be caused by a number of diseases, such as diabetes and hypoglycemia, or by some medications, such as those used to lower high blood pressure. Depression can also be caused by imbalances in the endocrine system. These are often experienced as premenstrual syndrome (PMS), postpartum blues, and mood fluctuations occurring after a hysterectomy or miscarriage. Some brain injuries also cause depression. Getting a physical checkup from a medical doctor will ensure that your physical health problems are being treated and will let you know if your depression may be caused partially by a medical problem.

Depression can cause you to lose all interest in personal grooming. But neglecting your personal grooming can also make you feel down. Taking care of your physical appearance may seem like a chore, but it is an effort that will help you feel better (unless you are dealing with a depressive illness that has physical or biochemical causes). When you clean up and dress up, your spirits usually go up. There are times when taking a shower, applying makeup, cologne, or perfume, putting on new clothes, and getting a haircut or new hairstyle may help you put on a brighter outlook on life as well.

It has been proven that physical exercise can raise your spirits by increasing the level of endorphins, brain chemicals that act as natural pain relievers. Whenever you exercise vigorously, your body releases endorphins, which can help you feel better emotionally. You may find immediate relief from darkened moods by engaging in some form of vigorous exercise that you enjoy. You may not feel like exercising when you start out, but once you choose to exercise, you unleash a natural high that can help you overcome your darkened mood.

PERSONAL EVALUATION

- When was the last time you had a complete medical evaluation by your doctor?
- Are you aware of any health conditions that are not being treated?
- Can you think of any physical changes or health conditions that might contribute to depression?
- Are you willing to take care of your physical health?
- Do you think you are depressed because of your physical condition and appearance, or are you

neglecting your physical condition and appearance because you are depressed?

- Are you willing to clean up and dress up in an attempt to feel better?
- What kind of exercise do you most enjoy?
- Are you willing to exercise vigorously to help yourself feel better?
- Do you feel unable to do vigorous exercise? What conditions make you feel unable? Is there any form of exercise you could do, given the conditions you must deal with?

ACTION

Make an appointment with your doctor for a complete physical if it has been more than a year since your last examination. Be sure to let your doctor know that you have been depressed and are looking for relief.

Take action to clean up and dress up, even if you are not planning to go out. Take a shower or even a bubble bath. Put on your favorite outfit, or go shopping for a new outfit and wear it home. Do the best you can to make yourself look your best, and smile at yourself in the mirror.

Let depression prompt you to exercise. Decide what form of vigorous exercise you most enjoy and have available to you. Give yourself fifteen to thirty minutes to exercise, even though you don't feel like it emotionally. You may find that once you get started, your mood will lift, and you will want to continue exercising. Try this today, and whenever you feel especially down, give yourself the fifteen-minute exercise treatment.

SUPPORT NOTES

Whatever the cause of the depression, your loved one probably won't be enthusiastic about doing the action steps for today. You can help by making the appointment for the medical evaluation and offering to take him to the appointment. Once he has medical confirmation that his physical condition will allow him to exercise, you can encourage him by offering to exercise with him or by helping him make arrangements for an exercise program he enjoys.

Do what you can to encourage him to care for his physical appearance without being critical of how he looks. He probably is struggling with low self-esteem and will not respond positively to criticism as an attempt to motivate him. Some conditions may make it very difficult to maintain even the most basic grooming routine. If he is dealing with a season of intense grief, perhaps it is not important for him to dress up. The somber dress may be a valid expression of grief. If his depression is caused by a physical condition, he could look his best every day, and it wouldn't make him feel better emotionally. Help him do what he can, note what helps and what does not, then keep these things in mind when he begins to define the contributing factors to his depression.

ENCOURAGEMENT

These external changes may or may not help you immediately. If they do, keep using them as part of your strategy to beat the blues. If you are unable to put them into practice for some reason, your willingness to give it your best effort will help you eventually by pointing you in the direction of deeper issues or conditions that need attention.

Nurturing a Healthy Mind

You can change your mind . . . and sometimes a change of mind can help you beat the blues. Has someone ever asked you why you seemed so depressed, and you answered that you had something on your mind? Often what is on your mind or in your mind contributes to having the blues. Today you will learn how to mentally unload some of what gets you down, plan to stop negative input, and begin to feed your mind on what is positive and uplifting.

There are probably things on your mind weighing you down. You may face stressful situations or problems demanding your attention. You may be grappling with losses while trying to establish a new way of life without whatever or whoever you have lost. You may have worries and fears that overshadow all other thoughts.

Having something on your mind that you can't seem to resolve may eventually leave you feeling depressed and hopeless. There are other cases where having the blues can make everything seem worse than it really is. A life that is generally good can seem dark and foreboding, and small difficulties take on enormous proportions when they are viewed through a mental haze of depression. Taking a look at what is on your mind and how you interpret it all can help you see whether your problems are contributing to your depression or your depression is exaggerating your problems.

You can easily get depressed if you carry a burden on your mind without moving toward resolving it. Some situations where that would be the case include worrying over things that are not in your power to change, worrying over problems that might arise but do not yet exist, worrying over someone else's life and carrying the burden of his responsibilities when he refuses to do so, or mulling over a problem that is in your power to change and yet not taking action to resolve it. In today's action step you will identify what is weighing on your mind and take steps toward relieving yourself of these burdens.

Your depression can also be influenced by what you feed your mind. If you feed on demoralizing, negative, or fatalistic ideas, you will spiral down into darker moods than your present ones. Even if your depression is not caused by these negative materials and ideas, they can accentuate the darkness you are experiencing. If you feed your mind on what is uplifting, hopeful, truthful, positive, and encouraging, your depression may not be cured, but you will have the advantage of a more positive outlook with which to deal with your darkened mood.

You have the power and responsibility to choose what you feed your mind. Some negative sources would be soap operas, pornography, conversation with negative people, music with depressing or vulgar lyrics, entertainment filled with violence or centered on fatalistic themes, negative religion where you are verbally and emotionally assaulted, and so on. Some positive sources for feeding your mind would be magazines with a commitment to positive themes (such as *Guideposts* or *Reader's Digest)*, motivational books and tapes, biographies of people who overcame tremendous obstacles in life, upbeat music with positive lyrics, religious experiences that are nonshaming, hopeful, and respectful, and so on.

PERSONAL EVALUATION

- What is on your mind that is weighing you down?
- What are you feeding your mind through what you see, hear, read, and think about?
- Of the things that feed your thoughts regularly, what negative influences do you see? What positive influences?
- Are you willing to adapt your mental diet to exclude the negative and increase the positive?

ACTION

Tell your support person what is weighing on your mind. As you do, the person should list every item. This list will help you separate your worries into specifics and reduce your feeling of being engulfed by what may seem like an ocean of problems.

Once you have listed all the things weighing on your mind, ask your support person to read the list back to you. For each item, answer these two questions:

1. Is this problem your responsibility, or is it someone else's problem? If it is yours, have your support person mark *M* (for mine) next to the item; if not, mark *S* (for someone else's).
2. Is this problem in your power to change? If it is, have your support person mark *Y* next to the item; if not, mark *N*.

Circle the items on your list that have both an *M* and a *Y*. These are your problems; the rest you need to let go of, unload, or release in some way. Draw a line through every item that either is not your problem or is not within your power to change. As you cross it off your list, try to mentally unload it from the burden you carry on your mind. Sometimes all it takes is the realization that there is really nothing you can do about the problem to be able to let go. Other times you may need to seek counseling to understand why you carry these burdens and how to release them.

For each circled item (your responsibility and within your power to change), discuss what you can do to try to resolve the problem or to get help to resolve the problem. Take some small step in that direction today.

If you find that you have been trying to carry numerous burdens that belong to someone else, consider whether you could benefit from getting help related to issues of codependency. Often codependency and depression go hand in hand, and recovery from codependency issues may alleviate your depression.

Ask your support person whether it seems that your problems are the source of your blues or your depressed mood is exaggerating problems in your mind. Carefully consider the response.

Decide what negative mental input you will eliminate, and take action to do so today.

Decide on three sources of positive input for your mind, feed on them today, and continue to give yourself positive input each day.

SUPPORT NOTES

As your friend lists what weighs on her mind, it can be a healing experience for you to validate that her concerns matter. Feel free to sympathize and affirm your sorrow that she is hurting so. Concentrate on listening carefully to her words and her emotions. However, it is important not to get so caught up in the emotion that you lose the ability to help her list her problems and burdens. She needs your help to unravel the jumble of emotions and issues into a list of separate problems. You will also help her see whether the burden is hers to bear and whether it is in her power to change. Don't get into an argument over this. If she insists that something is in her power to change, go ahead and decide what she can do to change it. At this point she may realize it is not in her power to change, even though she wishes that it were.

ENCOURAGEMENT

Choosing to change your mind in positive and healthy ways will help you beat the blues and more fully enjoy life in the future.

FOOD FOR THOUGHT

You are where you are, you are what you are because of what has gone into your mind. You can change where you are, you can change what you are by changing what goes into your mind.

—Zig Ziglar

Nourishing Your Spiritual Health

When you've got the blues, the invading darkness can reach to the depths of your being, even casting shadows over your spiritual life. There are many ways to nourish yourself spiritually that can offset some of the stress and anxiety associated with depression. Doing things that lift your spirits is a healthy part of an overall plan to beat the blues.

Here are some ways to nourish your spiritual health:

Pray. Prayer can take many therapeutic forms. Even if you are not sure about your relationship with God, you can still benefit from prayer.

If you don't know whether you believe in God, ask God to reveal Himself to you and help you. If He doesn't exist, you have nothing to lose. If He does exist, you may discover a powerful ally in your battle against depression.

Pour out your sorrows to God. The Bible says that God collects our tears in a bottle. You are invited to cast your cares upon God because He cares for you. Assume that God cares deeply about you, and pour out your heart before Him.

Give thanks. Even though you are troubled, there must be some things in life that you can be thankful for. Expressing thanks to God can elevate your perspective and lighten your mood.

Ask God for the specific things you need, including insight into what is causing your depression, resources to help you, and the ability to enjoy life again.

Surround yourself with beauty. Beauty, especially the beauty of nature, can be tremendously refreshing. Take time to relax amidst whatever natural beauty is available to you. Walking in the woods, strolling through a field of wildflowers, or sitting on the beach while watching the waves can nourish your spirit. Beauty can also be found in creative works of music and art. Expose yourself to what you find beautiful. Brighten up your surroundings with beautiful colors.

Meditate on things that are true and good. When you are battling the blues, it is easy to focus on all that is wrong with the world. Instead, try taking a few moments each day to quiet yourself, relax, and focus your mind on something that is right. Don't get involved in any type of meditation that empties your mind of all focused thought. When you are in a darkened mood, that kind of open-mindedness can lead you farther into darkness.

Be creative in the use of your talents. Use whatever gift of creative expression you have. If you sing, sing out your blues. If you draw or paint, use that medium to express yourself. If you have mechanical ability, be constructive and build something. If you write, compose a poem or song to express your feelings. Creative expression can give vent to deep emotions that you may not be able to get out any other way. You can also give yourself a sense of accomplishment.

You probably can think of other things unique to your spiritual experience that you know will nourish you spiritually. Now is not the time to deprive yourself. Find as many ways as possible to nourish yourself to the depth of your being.

PERSONAL EVALUATION

- Are you willing to pray? If not, why?
- Where do you have access to the beauty of nature? When is the next time you have available you could plan to get out into the beauty of nature?
- What is something good or true or right that you could meditate on in a quiet moment? (Think of positive quotes, good facts about your life, Bible verses, and so on.)
- What form of creative expression do you enjoy?

ACTION

Pray. In whatever way you can, call out to God to help you find your way out of depression. Your prayer can be as simple as this: "Dear God, please help me overcome this depression. Amen." Or you can use your prayer time to pour your heart out to God and tell Him all that is troubling you. Pray with the knowledge that God is on your side and wants to help you. Ask specifically for what you need. If you feel unable to pray for yourself, allow your support person to hold your hands and pray for you. The physical contact and the spiritual contact will do you good.

Plan a time in the near future to get out into the beauty of nature. If you can visit a place of beauty nearby, consider taking your daily walks there. Whenever you feel especially down, listen to beautiful music that soothes your spirit. Bring flowers into your home.

Before you go to sleep tonight, focus your mind on one thing that is good or true or right. Try to keep that thought uppermost in your mind until you go to sleep. Make a practice of this throughout the course of your journey.

Express yourself creatively in some way, even if no one else ever hears or sees what you create.

SUPPORT NOTES

Spiritual issues can be a mine field when someone is depressed. Your loved one may doubt the existence of God or at least doubt the goodness of any God who would leave him in such despair. When someone is depressed, he often feels exceedingly sinful or guilt-ridden and assumes that God would not receive his prayers. He may also vent his hostilities at God.

You need to be compassionate and allow your loved one to be honest about how he feels regarding spiritual issues, even if that offends your spiritual sensibilities. Now is not the time to point out where he falls short in his spiritual life. If you have a deep relationship with God you wish he could share, then use your private time of prayer to seek God's help on his behalf rather than try to preach to him right now.

Remind him that his depression also colors his perspective regarding spiritual issues, and his spiritual life may not be as bleak as it seems. Encourage him to do whatever he can to nourish himself spiritually. Perhaps you can offer him whatever access you have to things that can bring beauty and light into his dark world.

ENCOURAGEMENT

Spiritual strength can uphold you when it seems that all other strength is spent.

Strengthening Relationships that Lift You Up

Human relationships, especially those within the family, have a forceful impact on your life. There are relationships that tear you down and others that build you up. When you've got the blues, you need to strengthen relationships that build you up. These are the relationships from which you will draw hope, courage, strength, and support when you are down and while you move back to health. You need to learn to nurture these uplifting relationships because they will be vital to your recovery.

The relationships that have power to tear you down may be an important clue to your depression. There are relationships within family systems that can leave you feeling trapped, locked into certain roles or situations that overwhelm you. There are love-hate relationships that constantly stir up conflicting emotions. There are abusive relationships where you are being abused or being abusive that evoke deep feelings of shame and degradation without much hope of breaking the destructive cycle. Any relationship that is destructive or degrading to your human dignity or that of the other person—but seems impossible to break free of—can lead to depression.

These types of destructive relational patterns are

best dealt with under the care of a professional therapist or counselor who understands the dynamics of family systems. If you recognize that your depression may be related to feeling trapped in dysfunctional relationships, you would do well to seek the help of a counselor. You probably should not try to cope with these issues on your own. What you can do on your own is to strengthen relationships with people who lift you up. You will rely more on their support while you move toward getting help to heal any destructive relationships.

These uplifting relationships need to be nurtured so that the other persons will continue to lend you support over the course of time and to show appreciation. By respecting these important relationships, you will also gain respect for yourself. There are some basic things you can do, even in your state of depression, that will nurture these relationships rather than exhaust the support being offered.

Here are some things you can do to strengthen these relationships:

Don't label a person in a supportive relationship as your savior. If you see one person as being the only one who can rescue you, the person will naturally draw away from such an overwhelming burden. Even though you need help during this season of life, you cannot transfer full responsibility for your life to another person and expect the relationship to last. Instead of assigning someone the role of savior, accept whatever role the individual can realistically play as part of your support network.

Be willing to face your problems and do whatever you can to help yourself. When you are willing to do as much as you can to help yourself, even if that is severely limited by the symptoms of your depression, others will be more willing to do whatever they can to help you, too.

Express your appreciation and gratitude. Don't assume that because you are depressed and feel desperately needy, people should be obligated to go out of their way to take care of you. If people give of themselves, let them know you appreciate their time, effort, involvement, and whatever else they give you. Remember to say thank you for what they try to do to help you, even if it doesn't make your pain go away.

Let them know whenever they have a positive impact on your life. Being around someone who is depressed can become quite discouraging when the moods don't seem to improve. Whenever people have a positive impact on you, tell them so. They may not be able to see how they are affecting you from your countenance.

Respect their limitations and boundaries. Don't expect them to give more than they are able of their time, finances, emotions, or anything else. Healthy people have boundaries—limits they set in relationships and life-style—that keep them balanced and nourished. Healthy people are probably the ones who are most uplifting to others. To stay healthy, they sometimes have to say no. When they do say no to something you feel you need from them, don't overreact. Instead, turn to others on your list of uplifting people, and see if they can help you in that particular way.

PERSONAL EVALUATION

- Do you think you may need to seek help to deal with the effects of destructive relationships that tear you down? Are you willing to do so? If not, why?
- Are there any items listed as ways to strengthen uplifting relationships that you find difficult? Place a check next to any of these relational skills you need to work on.
- Are you willing to make changes in your relational style to strengthen relationships with people who lift you up?

ACTION

Ask your support person to divide a sheet of paper into two columns: "People Who Tear You Down" and "People Who Lift You Up."

Begin naming people you have relationships with every day, and tell your support person which column they belong in. Start with your immediate family, extended family, friends, work associates, support network, and others. Keep going until you have at least five people in the uplifting column.

Keep the other list available in case you later decide to seek counseling for relational issues.

Focus your attention on your relationships with these five people. Then have your support person read over the list of ways you can strengthen these relationships. After each item is read, tell your support person how you are willing to act to strengthen your relationship with each person in that particular way. Note one way that you have not acted to strengthen your relationship with each person on your list, and do something today to change that. The easiest way would be to contact the people on your list and say thank you for the specific ways they have uplifted you.

SUPPORT NOTES

This type of evaluation can become the basis for self-condemnation instead of a step toward improving relationships. When someone is depressed, she may become so focused on what she is doing wrong, she loses sight of what she can do to change. Your role is to help her focus on making positive changes rather than condemn herself for not being the world's best friend. Remind her that she may be dealing with an illness that makes her *unable* to relate as well as she would like. Also remind her that she is loved by those who uplift her and she will not always be as needy as she is now.

She may also get sidetracked into focusing on

the relationships that are destructive. Unless you are a licensed therapist, you are not equipped to unravel the destructive cords of her relational life. Don't let her get off track from today's assignment. Instead, help her focus on looking for the relationships that can have a positive impact. If she cannot identify individuals who are uplifting, try to help her in the process by suggesting people you see as willing to be of help if they were allowed. Include professionals who would be a part of the support network (counselors, support group leaders, doctors, etc.).

ENCOURAGEMENT

When you make the effort to contribute what you can to a relationship, you will usually find the person on the other side becomes more willing to give as well.

Letting Go of Assumptions and Biases

Many contributing influences may play a part in the cause and cure of your depression. The moment you assume you know precisely what the cause is, to the exclusion of other possible contributing influences, you close the door to possible avenues of help. When your personal biases close your mind to possible solutions, you may block the way to relief and lock yourself into depression. Letting go of assumptions and biases can be the key to discovering what is causing your problems and what needs to be done to remedy the situation.

You might have adopted your assumptions on the basis of limited information available to you. For instance, if you were not aware (as many people are not) that depression can be caused by purely physical conditions, you would assume your depression was an emotional, relational, or spiritual problem. You could exhaust yourself trying to make changes in these areas that would do nothing to resolve the source of depression if it was physical or biochemical. Gaining new information can open the door to new possibilities for healing if you are willing to be open-minded and relieve your frustration.

You might have formed your assumptions on the basis of your biases. Depending on your particular focus in life, you might be biased against certain forms of treatment or perspectives regarding the causes and cures of depression. Perhaps you have seen someone abuse some form of treatment or heard about harmful side effects from medication, and you concluded neither was an option for you. You might have been taught that all depression is a matter of choosing to give in to despair, and the only way to get over it is to determine to think more positively or perhaps to pray more faithfully. Perhaps you believe that if people say they can't control their moods, they are being irresponsible, and so you struggle to control your moods as best you can. Your bias makes it such that admitting what may be the truth about your condition seems like admitting personal failure.

Beware of your biases. Sometimes you develop a bias as a form of protection from the very issues at the root of your depression. In your attempt to protect yourself from painful memories that might have been buried as the result of a traumatic experience, you may irrationally avoid any issue that threatens to touch on areas of pain in your past. You may disavow the possibility that abuse or victimization could have anything to do with your depression because you perceive your past life as near perfect. You may not realize that many people who have been severely victimized or traumatized have no conscious memory of the event. Rather, they experience unexplained depression, anxiety attacks, and chronic physical ailments that defy explanation. They may also tend toward focusing attention anywhere other than the issues associated with the real problem. In this way, your biases may act as defense mechanisms that exclude accurate indicators of your issues or treatment methods moving in the direction of the true problem.

It is to your advantage to let go of your assumptions and put aside your biases for the time being. Consider the new information you will receive during the remainder of your journey, and consider new possibilities that may lead you to the resolution of things contributing to your depression. You need not give up your values and beliefs; just reevaluate your problem from a broader perspective.

Over the next few days you will learn about various kinds of depression and influences known to contribute to depression. Your willingness to let go of your assumptions and biases will allow you to better evaluate your situation and come up with a personalized plan for recovery.

PERSONAL EVALUATION

- What have you assumed to be the contributing factors related to your depression?
- Whom do you blame when you try to figure out why you are so depressed?
- What biases do you have that would cause you to exclude the possibility of certain causes or cures of depression?

- What possible options for treatment have you excluded as being options for you? Why?
- Are you willing to let go of your previous assumptions, for the time being, in order to open yourself to new possibilities?

ACTION

Tell your support person what you assume to be the factors contributing to your depression. Ask the person to list them.

Tell your support person what other possible contributing factors you assume *not* to have an influence on your bout with the blues. (Note: You may not be aware of any other factors or may not have any assumptions. If that is the case, skip this part.)

Tell your support person any types of treatment you have ruled out and why. Ask the person to list each one along with your reasons or a list of obstacles that you see as being prohibitive. For example, you exclude the possibility of counseling because you don't know a counselor you can trust or because you are afraid it will be too expensive to continue as long as necessary to deal with the issues. Or you exclude medical treatment because you don't believe a medical problem can make you feel the way you do emotionally.

It is especially important to be thorough in listing your objections, hesitations, and reasons you believe particular forms of treatment to be off-limits for you. As you explore the kind of depression you may be dealing with, you may find that one of the treatment options you've excluded is appropriate for the type of symptoms you are experiencing. At that point you will be farther along if you already have a list of specific obstacles to overcome on your way to getting the help you need.

Your last action step today is most important. It is the act of choice. Will you choose to acknowledge the assumptions and biases you have identified but to also set them aside for the remainder of the journey? At that time you will have more information with which to reassess these beliefs and either confirm or adapt them. The choice is yours.

SUPPORT NOTES

Your loved one's assumptions and biases are important to him. He has probably struggled to figure out what the problem is and how he can get better. Be respectful of his thoughts, even if you disagree. In fact, you need to keep your assumptions and biases out of the discussion. Your goal is to help him feel accepted and safe enough to honestly express these thoughts. Do not argue with him or criticize. Just listen, ask questions to clarify the information, and write down the lists and reasons he gives you. Your desire to see him open up to new possibilities must not be pressured upon him. Give him the respect, acceptance, and freedom to choose his own path toward health.

Are You Dealing with Normal Depression?

Over the next few days you will learn about the various kinds of depression and the differences between them so you can see if they may be part of your problem. You will not identify with each of them, but knowing what is not the problem will also help you narrow down your focus to find the help appropriate for you.

You are probably familiar with what is called *normal depression*. Normal depression is the normal response you may have to overwhelming stress or loss. This type of depression is directly related to sources of stress that are identifiable. Sometimes normal depression lasts only a short time after a particularly stressful event and may be fairly mild. It can also linger for long seasons of time and be severe enough to warrant hospitalization, especially if you become suicidal.

Normal depression is linked to the grieving process you must go through when you experience loss or disappointment. A season of depression during grieving is actually healthy, even though you are experiencing deep sorrow and anguish. If you move through the grief process without getting stuck, you will naturally come out of the depression and resume a normal life. If you get stuck somewhere in grief and stop moving out of loss, you may find yourself overcome by depression.

Normal depression can also come from being stressed out. Any change in life, good or bad, will create stress. You can experience stress-related depression after completing a major life goal or being fired from your job. When your level of stress is high, it takes its toll on your body, mind, and emotions. Living with a high stress level over a prolonged period of time can lead to depression and exhaustion.

PERSONAL EVALUATION

When answering the questions about loss, include all types of loss: death; divorce; the loss of a job, friendships, finances, direction in life, innocence, the image you had of yourself or your marriage; the loss of an addiction (it would be a positive loss, but you still experience the pain of losing something that helped you cope); the loss of a beloved pet; and so on.

- What losses have you experienced recently (within the last year)?
- What have you lost in your lifetime that still grieves you when you think about it? It could be something as simple as losing a contest that was important to you as a child or as complex as feeling that you lost your childhood because of growing up in a dysfunctional home.

ACTION

Ask your support person to list your recent and lifetime losses.

Read this list of stress factors, and mark any that have happened to you in the last year. This list is not comprehensive; it is given to spark your thinking. Add to this list any other stressors that add to your overall level of stress.

- Death of a spouse
- Death of immediate family member
- Divorce or separation in your marriage
- Divorce or separation of parents
- Move to a new location
- Addition to your family
- Family member moved away from home
- Completed major goal (such as graduation)
- Loss of job
- New job
- Financial difficulties
- Purchase or sale of a home
- Birth of a baby
- Long work hours
- Pressures and deadlines you are racing to meet

Rate your overall stress level on a scale of one to ten (one means that you don't feel stressed at all, five means a moderate level of stress, and ten means that you feel ready to explode).

SUPPORT NOTES

The purpose of today's journey is to determine if there are some identifiable stressors that would normally cause your loved one to experience some level of depression. You are not supposed to help her work through her loss, nor is it your job to tell her how to reduce her level of stress. The goal is to help her see if her blues may be related to normal depression caused by identifiable stressors. If she seems like she needs to talk about her losses and the associated pain, move through the questions quickly and then spend time listening to her. If there is a high level of stress in her life, it may be a relief to her to realize that perhaps anyone would have cause to be depressed if he had been through the recent experiences she had.

ENCOURAGEMENT

Normal depression can be your body's way of shutting down so you can deal with the stress you've had to deal with. Although it is painful, it is a part of the normal process of growing, adapting, and changing that will help you go forward with your life.

Are You Dealing with a Depressive Illness?

It may be hard to believe your emotional pain and mental confusion can be caused by a physical condition, but that is proven to be true. There are many times when depression is caused by a physical condition: a chemical imbalance in the brain, a hormonal imbalance, a secondary symptom of disease, a brain injury, or a substance in the body (such as medication or alcohol). For the purposes of this journey these forms of depression, caused primarily by physical conditions, will be called *depressive illness*.

Chemical Imbalance In a booklet prepared by Merrell Dow Pharmaceuticals, Inc., Joseph Talley, M.D., and Beverly Mead, M.D., call depression "a common illness, one of the most common in all of medicine." They explain that many misconceptions regarding depression are commonly held, saying, "We used to think that unusual depression was due to some hidden unhappiness or conflict in a person's life. We now know that many otherwise healthy people who have no reason to be unhappy become depressed, too."

Research by Talley and Mead has shown that much depression unrelated to identifiable stressors is caused by a deficiency of one or two biochemicals that carry brain impulses from one nerve ending in the brain to the next. They deliver messages across the synapse between nerves, then jump back to the nerve they came from. These brain messengers are called neurotransmitters. When there are enough neurotransmitters to carry impulses from one nerve ending to the next, you are able to feel fine. But when there is a deficiency of these neurotransmitters, the result is what we commonly recognize as depression.

Doctors Talley and Mead state,

> When this deficiency occurs in a person's arms or legs or trunk of the body, various kinds of loss of motion or limitation of function can occur. **When the deficiency of messengers occurs in the brain, the result is Depression.** . . . In other words, we now say that depression is caused by a chemical imbalance in the brain, and anti-depression medication helps return brain chemistry to normal.

There are two primary categories of depression with biochemical origins: major depression and manic depression. Major depression is characterized by recurrent bouts of depression and accompanied by other physical symptoms, most notably sleep disturbances. Manic depression (also called bipolar depression because the person swings between two alternating poles) is characterized by extreme mood swings between high manic moods and extreme low depressed moods. Both conditions are thought to be influenced by genetic factors. However, research is more conclusive that manic depression is hereditary.

Hormonal Imbalance   Several forms of hormonal imbalance can have emotional symptoms associated with depression. They include thyroid conditions, conditions related to the endocrine system and, most commonly recognized, the hormonal fluctuations experienced during the female menstrual and reproductive cycle. Serious depression is reported by up to 30 percent of women several days to a week before and/or just after the start of menstruation. In times past the condition was largely dismissed as being purely emotional or imaginary. In recent years the condition we know as PMS (premenstrual syndrome) has been legitimized and successfully treated medically as well as with the use of exercise. Also, it is common to experience depressive illness related to hormonal imbalance at menarche (when a girl first begins menstruating), during menopause, after a miscarriage, after the birth of a child, or after an abortion or a tubal ligation.

In these cases the symptoms of depression are caused by fluctuations in the hormonal balance between the ovarian hormones, estrogen and progesterone. Drugs that block the release of these hormones have proven to relieve depression and other related physical discomforts. However, using contraceptive pills may cause depression in some women because of the way they affect the hormonal balance.

Secondary Symptom of Disease   Depression is occasionally a secondary symptom of another disease such as hypoglycemia or diabetes. Although rare, it is important to note for two reasons. First, a bout with the blues that seems unrelated to your circumstances or stress level may be a helpful indicator leading to the discovery of a medical condition that requires treatment. Second, if your depression is one of the rare cases that is caused as a secondary symptom of disease, you would do well to consider this possibility to spare yourself the frustration, time, and effort trying to figure out why you are so depressed.

Brain Injury   Depression can result from a brain injury. If there is physical injury to the brain, it can affect whatever brain functions are conducted by the injured area: emotional perceptions, memory, and thought processes.

Substance in the Body   Alcohol and many other recreational drugs act as depressants in the body. Prescription drugs can also have depression as a possible side effect, which has been seen to be the case with medication routinely used to reduce high blood pressure. If you are taking any type of medication or recreational drug, particularly if you are addicted to alcohol, your depression may be one of the side effects. It can be a deadly combination. There is a high correlation to the incidence of suicide in people who are depressed and addicted to alcohol.

PERSONAL EVALUATION

- Does your depression occur unrelated to whether your circumstances are good or bad?
- Is there a history of depression or manic depression in your family?
- Are you certain (having had a physical examination by a doctor) that you do not have another disease that may have depression as a secondary condition?
- Have you had any head or brain injury that occurred previous to your bout with the blues?
- What medications and mood-altering substances are you using?

ACTION

Here are some symptoms and factors associated with depressive illness. Circle Y (yes) or N (no) to note whether it applies to you. If you do not know the answer for sure, put a question mark over the Y/N.

You experience lowered moods unrelated to whether circumstances are good or bad .... Y/N

You experience sleep disturbances .... Y/N

You have a family history of depression (symptoms of depression have been seen in parents, grandparents, siblings, aunts and uncles) .... Y/N

You have significant mood swings from extreme highs to extreme lows that are unre-

lated to whether circumstances are good or
bad . . . . Y/N

*If you answered yes to any of the preceding, there
is the possibility you are dealing with a chemical
imbalance in the brain that may cause your depression.*

You are at a place in your menstrual cycle
where you typically experience depression   Y/N
You have recently experienced a miscarriage,
an abortion, or a tubal ligation . . . . Y/N
You are going through menopause . . . . Y/N
You are using a prescription contraceptive
that may cause depression as a side effect   Y/N
You have a thyroid condition that is not be-
ing treated properly . . . . Y/N

*If you answered yes to any of the preceding, you
may have a hormonal imbalance.*

You have diabetes, hypoglycemia, or another
medical condition known to cause depres-
sion in some people . . . . Y/N
You have had a head injury, which coincides
with the onset of your depression . . . . Y/N
You use alcohol . . . . Y/N
You use marijuana and/or other recreational
drugs . . . . Y/N
You use prescription medication that can
cause depression as a side effect in some peo-
ple . . . . Y/N

Enlist the help of your support person to find the information you need to turn your question marks into definite "yes" or "no" statements.

SUPPORT NOTES

Today's journey requires focused thought and concentration, which may be difficult for your friend. Help him as much as possible by including any information you have about his condition, medical and family history. Don't let him guess or make assumptions in answering the questions in the action step. If he is not absolutely sure, encourage him to use the question mark. Then take the lead in helping him get the information necessary to find a definite answer. You may even need to do the research for him. The important thing is that these questions are answered definitively.

ENCOURAGEMENT

By objectively considering the possible physical and medical causes of your condition, you will gain a fuller picture of what you are dealing with and what needs to be done to help you feel better. I encourage you to be honest with yourself about the use of alcohol and other mood-altering drugs, even though you may strongly resist facing the thought of giving them up. No one is demanding you give them up now. But you need to get beyond your denial in order to see clearly what may be making you miserable.

Are You Dealing with Negative Attitudes and Beliefs?

Some depression is brought on by years of living with negative attitudes and self-destructive beliefs. These attitudes and beliefs shape your choices, behavior, and relational style and determine the consequences that come back to you. It has been said, "You can be as happy as you make up your mind to be." Although that may be somewhat simplistic (especially if you are dealing with a form of depressive illness), to a large degree, your level of happiness is a choice you make. That choice begins with your attitudes and beliefs.

Developing positive attitudes and true beliefs, which uphold self-respect, will help you face whatever difficulties life brings your way. It will even be easier to deal with depressive illness if you have learned to practice positive attitudes and have a firm foundation of truth to uphold you during your depression. Negative attitudes and faulty beliefs alone are enough to depress you. If they are added to other contributing factors, they can magnify the problems considerably. The good news is that you can change your attitudes and beliefs and, in so doing, change your level of happiness.

The first step in correcting any problem is to identify it and admit that it exists. Today you will look at some negative attitudes and beliefs that can contribute to depression. You may also think of others particular to you that you want to add. Remember, the purpose in identifying them is not to condemn yourself. The purpose is to make corrections that can lead to relief.

Here are some negative attitudes that lead to depression:

"The world owes me!" If you have been deprived, hurt, or abused, you may have the attitude the world owes you or particular people owe you. This attitude leads to failure to accept responsibility for your own recovery, conflict in relationships, lowered productivity, and resentment. We live in a broken world where life isn't fair. No one will ever be able to make up to you precisely what you feel is owed. The weight of these growing accounts you keep of wrongs suffered will eventually become depressing. The only way for these emotionally weighty debts to be reduced is for you to cancel them.

"It's their fault." An attitude that tends toward blaming others for your feelings or your failings can leave you depressed. You may find yourself saying things like, "He makes me miserable," or "I can't do anything to make my life more enjoyable while I have to live with her." Blaming others leaves you in the powerless position of a victim. It also relieves you of responsibility for your emotional state, behavior, and success or failure. When you choose to stop blaming others for making you miserable, you accept responsibility for your life and become free to take steps to make yourself happier.

"I can make it on my own." Isolation is a choice usually born of a need for self-protection. This attitude that tells others to keep their distance can leave you lonely and depressed. Every human being needs to be loved and needs relationships with other people. You might have been neglected, hurt, and disappointed in ways that led you to develop an attitude of fierce independence. Healthy interdependence allows you enough control to make sure you are not left at the mercy of others but also enough relationship to nourish your need to be loved.

"If only . . ." Living in the past and allowing your life to revolve around regrets are depressing. You can choose to face the future and realize that whatever has happened in your past can become either a stumbling block or a stepping-stone, depending on how you choose to see it. You can always learn from your experiences and make changes that lead to a brighter future.

"I deserve to be miserable." Taking on the martyr's attitude makes your state of depression into a relational weapon as well as a badge. You may find that you wear your moods to remind people of how much you have been through and to get them to be more lenient in their expectations of you. When you are depressed, the family may be more loving and patient. Some people become emotionally reliant on their state of depression to manipulate others into treating them better. This attitude may give you some small payback, but it leaves you depressed. How much better it is to learn to give and receive love without having to make people feel sorry for you in order to receive the loving response you need.

"I can never forgive them (or myself)." Unforgiveness, bitterness, and resentment can take over your life, leaving you emotionally exhausted and depressed. If you choose to forgive others, you are not saying what they did was acceptable. You are simply releasing yourself from having to carry the weight of emotion focused on what they did to you. You are handing the burden of avenging the wrong into the hands of God so that you can get on with your life. If you are holding unforgiveness against yourself, you must find absolution so that you don't stay miserable just because that is what you think you deserve.

"I'll never have enough." Being ungrateful for what you have is a downer. When you always see your glass as half empty instead of half full, you may choose to be depressed. When you learn to see life in a large enough perspective to appreciate what you do have and express gratitude, you will find joy that is unknown to those who persist in an attitude of ingratitude.

Here are some beliefs that lead to depression:

"I can't make a difference." You believe there is nothing you can do to make a real difference in the outcome of things or to contribute anything of eternal value.

"I am worthless." You do not see yourself as being created by God as someone who is unique and valuable. Instead, you see yourself as being worthless in society's scheme of things.

"I am shamefully flawed." Unhealthy shame is based on the belief there is something terribly wrong with you at the core of your being. It is believing not that you *made* a mistake but that you *are* a mistake.

"I am powerless." You may not see any way for you to change particular situations. You may also believe you are powerless to change your attitudes and beliefs. You may believe that since life has been rotten to you, you are obligated to be miserable. You might have been overpowered so much in your life that being a victim and being characterized by the quality of powerlessness have become a part of your identity.

PERSONAL EVALUATION

- How do you see your attitudes and beliefs relating to your depression?
- Have you ever experienced a change in attitude or belief that affected your life in a positive way?
- Would you be willing to take steps to change your attitudes and beliefs if you knew that would help you beat the blues?

ACTION

Rate yourself on a scale of one to ten for how much you hold these attitudes and beliefs that can contribute to depression (one means you never hold this attitude or belief, five means you have this attitude or belief sometimes, and ten means you hold it most or all of the time). List any other negative attitudes you see that may contribute to your depression, and rate yourself on them, too.

If you are willing to have a gauge of whether you perceive yourself as others perceive you, ask your support person to rate you on each one in the same way. If you don't want the person's perspective, you don't have to do this part of the step. If you do want the input, go over your ratings together and compare. You can choose to change your rating if you like after comparing the two perspectives. Rate yourself on the following:

                                            RATING

"The world owes me!" . . . . _____

"It's their fault." . . . . _____

"I can make it on my own." . . . . _____

"If only . . ." . . . . _____

"I deserve to be miserable." . . . . _____

"I can never forgive them (or myself)." . . . _____

"I'll never have enough." . . . . _____

"I can't make a difference." . . . . _____

"I am worthless." . . . . _____

"I am shamefully flawed." . . . . _____

"I am powerless." . . . . _____

SUPPORT NOTES

Your loved one may not be seeing herself realistically and could possibly benefit from comparing your perspective to her own. If she feels comfortable enough to do this part of the action step, be courteous but honest. Think of specific instances that led you to your evaluation so that she doesn't lapse into feeling persecuted or attacked. Do not lecture her or try to persuade her to change. Simply offer your perspective if she asks. If she doesn't ask for your perspective but her evaluation seems out of touch with reality, tell her your observations but don't try to make her change her evaluation.

ENCOURAGEMENT

Facing the possibility that you may be partially responsible for your depression because of your attitudes and beliefs can give you a powerful new option for change. Your courage in facing this possibility honestly may open the door to a healthier and happier way of life.

Are You Dealing with Spiritual or Relational Issues?

Several spiritual and relational issues can contribute to depression. Consider whether they could be part of your problem.

Spiritual Issues

Alienation from God. You may feel distance between yourself and God. Perhaps you feel unworthy to be accepted by God, or you are at war with God for your own reasons. Either way, this alienation can be a burden to you.

An area of sin you cannot break free from. Sin means "to fall short of the mark." Violating your set of moral values can be quite distressing. That is especially true when you try to do what is right and find you continue to do the very things you don't believe in and don't want to do because they violate your moral standards.

Demonic influence or oppression. Beliefs vary widely regarding the influence of unseen spiritual forces. There are some who believe depression can be caused or aggravated by being involved with the occult or experiencing ritualistic abuse.

Living a double life. When you believe one set of values and make a public commitment to them but secretly live another life, it can create a great deal of stress. That can also happen if you present yourself dishonestly to the people near you and you have to keep up pretenses. Recent news accounts told of a man who lived a triple life. He was married to three different women at the same time; none of the wives knew of the others' existence.

Relational Issues There are times when relational problems and cycles will leave you feeling stuck and depressed. Living in a situation where there is abuse, behavior that violates your conscience, neglect, or betrayal can bring about depression until you find a way to resolve your relational issues and move on with your life.

PERSONAL EVALUATION

- How do you think your spiritual life could possibly contribute to your depression?
- How do you think relational problems could possibly contribute to your depression?

ACTION

Rate yourself on a scale of one to ten for how much you think each of these spiritual issues may contribute to your depression (one means very little, five means you think it may have a moderate influence, and ten means you see it as a key contributing influence). List any other spiritual issues you see that may contribute to your depression, and rate them in the same way. Rate yourself on the following:

RATING

Alienation from God . . . . _____
An area of sin you cannot break free from

. . . . _____
Demonic influence or oppression . . . . . . _____
Living a double life . . . . _____
Other spiritual issue . . . . _____

To gauge the impact of relational issues on your depression, list the names of the people with whom you are having difficulties you believe could be contributing to your depression. Give your support person the list, and describe the problem in each relationship. Ask your support person to write one or two sentences after each name to summarize what you see the problem to be. Then read the whole thing together to be sure both of you clearly understand the problems in the relationships.

SUPPORT NOTES

Spiritual issues touch to the core of a person's being and may be considered quite personal. Your loved one may not feel comfortable discussing spiritual issues with you. If that is the case, respect his privacy in this matter. If he wants to talk about spiritual issues, try to be a source of comfort to him in whatever way you can without preaching.

If in discussing relational issues, he confides that he is being abused or that he is in danger from someone, take immediate action to get him appropriate help and protection. Don't leave him in the situation.

ENCOURAGEMENT

Once you have identified spiritual and relational issues that may be contributing to your depression, you are well on your way to being able to resolve those issues in a positive way.

Unraveling a Mystery Depression

A *mystery depression* is a term I use to describe depression that doesn't fit neatly into the category of depressive illness, negative attitudes or beliefs, or identifiable spiritual and relational issues. If you have gone through the exercises for the last few days and feel as though you're grasping at straws because none of the possible contributing factors seem to apply to your situation, you are dealing with a mystery that needs to be solved.

Sometimes depression can be an indicator of repressed trauma. Perhaps a factor contributing to your depression is something deeply hidden. It may be something so terrible you are trying to forget it or push it out of your mind. It may be something that was so deeply devastating your mind has hidden it away from you. There are cases where repressed trauma results in depression. These cases often involve some form of extreme violence and/or sexual abuse.

Statistics show that one of four girls and one of eight boys are abused sexually by the age of eighteen. In the past decade there has been a 943 percent increase in sexual abuse cases. Sexual abuse is tremendously shameful and can leave you living in hiding, bearing the pain of what has happened, and harboring the fear of telling anyone about it. This kind of prolonged secrecy, shame, and untreated pain leads to depression.

A letter to the editor of a popular women's magazine was from a woman who had silently suffered from depression off and on over twenty-five years. She had been raped by a public official in her small town. She bottled up her secret and painful emotions inside, afraid that no one would believe her. After reading an article about the ongoing effects of rape, the woman found courage to tell her husband what had happened to her. She finally received help for the emotional pain that had accumulated inside and found her depression relieved.

If you are hiding a terrible secret, or if you have no recollection of abuse but periods of time are missing from your memory, your mystery depression may be a cry for help from within. If you cannot find identifiable causes and solutions for your depression by completing this journey, it would be in your best interest to seek professional help. Perhaps you have had an experience that was so traumatic your mind completely blocked it out from your consciousness. If that is the case, a good therapist with a proven track record working with repressed trauma and those who have been victims of abuse can help you determine if your mystery depression may be a clue to something deeper needing to be resolved.

PERSONAL EVALUATION

- Are you aware of anything traumatic or abusive that happened to you or someone you love that you are trying not to think about?
- Are there large gaps in your memory about your life?
- Are you willing to consider the possibility of a repressed trauma contributing to your depression if you are unable to identify any other contributing factors?

ACTION

Do you have any reason to believe that your depression might be partially caused by some experience of abuse or trauma?

If it seems to be a possibility, ask your support person to help you find a therapist who can give you professional assistance in exploring the possibility.

SUPPORT NOTES

If your loved one is at a loss concerning the source of her depression, encourage her to get a diagnosis from a therapist who specializes in dealing with repressed trauma. There is nothing to lose. Strong resistance to the idea may indicate a problem she is afraid to face.

If your loved one begins to remember flashes of

traumatic or shameful experiences, reaffirm your acceptance, love, and support. Do not try to handle the problem on your own. Get professional help. If she tells you about specific acts of abuse or identifies her abuser, listen compassionately. If she is living in a dangerous situation, take steps immediately to protect her. Never minimize or cover up abuse. Get help.

ENCOURAGEMENT

If you have been abused, there is treatment available to help you face the pain and shame of what happened to you and recover to enjoy life again.

Time for Laughter and Relaxing

You have probably heard that laughter is the best medicine. When it comes to beating the blues, laughter isn't always the best medicine, but it will always make you feel better while you find the best medicine for whatever is causing your depression. Medical research has shown that laughter actually has therapeutic effects within the body. Laughing speeds up your heart rate, releases endorphins into your system (which act as natural pain relievers), and relieves stress. Do yourself a favor. Give yourself a healthy dose of laughter.

So far, this journey has been a lot of work, requiring concentration and self-reflection. You need to take a day or so to let yourself laugh and relax before moving on to develop and implement your personal recovery plan. Today this will be a conscious effort. I hope that seeing you can choose to bring laughter into your life will encourage you to make it a daily practice.

In the midst of a difficult time of life, there is always room for a little laughter. You can make choices that bring laughter into your life, even during times of depression or grieving. You can make a conscious effort to look for what is humorous and to discover things that are funny. Even if the laughter is only for a moment, it can be tremendously refreshing.

Vic Gold, in *The Washingtonian*, said, "What makes us cry is simple to describe. What makes us laugh is harder to pin down. Like the taste of celery, it defies description." It may be harder to pin down but try. Think of things that can make you laugh: episodes of "I Love Lucy!"; a ride on a roller coaster; the Three Stooges; Laurel and Hardy movies; a book by Erma Bombeck; a comedy routine by Bill Cosby; and so on.

PERSONAL EVALUATION

Think of times when you laughed very hard. You may have to think back some, but keep thinking until you come up with some good memories of laughter and fun.

- Which people or entertainers have made you laugh in the past?
- What kinds of activities have you enjoyed that actually have made you laugh out loud?

ACTION

Just for today, try to put aside the work you are doing to beat the blues, and make yourself laugh.

Tell your support person the story of a time when you laughed very hard and what made you laugh.

Tell your support person two activities you have enjoyed that have made you laugh out loud and the names of entertainers, comedians, movies, and books you think are funny.

Choose an activity that you consider fun. Go out and do it. Maybe go to an amusement park or go waterskiing.

Rent a video from the comedy section of your local video store. I recommend "Bill Cosby Himself" (it is especially enjoyable if you have small children; the sketch he does on parenting is hysterical) or episodes of "Candid Camera."

Find television reruns of "I Love Lucy!" or other comedies, and watch them.

Get a book from the comedy section of your local bookstore and read it out loud to your support person, or take turns reading it to each other.

As you choose funny material, look for material that is respectable and respectful. Stay away from material that is vulgar or makes you laugh by demeaning someone else. This type of comedy may make you laugh, but you may also feel a tinge of guilt if the material offends your conscience. If the material is vulgar and degrading, it will not have the positive, lasting effect you need.

As your journey continues, take a few moments each day to delight in something funny.

Support Notes

Your loved one may not feel like laughing and may drag his feet at first in the attempt to think of anything funny or tell you a funny story. If that is the case, take the lead. Go to the video store, and get something that will make him laugh. All he needs to do is to agree to watch. Once he is laughing a little, it may lift him up to the point that he can find some of the laughter in his own soul.

Encouragement

Your willingness to entertain yourself and make yourself laugh will pay off. You will find yourself refreshed and better prepared to complete your journey.

Sorting Out Contributing Influences

Today you will review what you have discovered over the course of your journey and identify all the possible contributing influences you may be dealing with. Once you have done this, you will learn how to go about handling each possibility appropriately.

PERSONAL EVALUATION

Go back to Day 12 and note which losses you may need to grieve and what factors are contributing to a high level of stress in your life.

Go back to Day 13 and note which symptoms and factors associated with depressive illness you identified as applying to you. By now you should have been able to answer yes or no for the items you weren't sure of and noted with a question mark. If you still are not sure of some items, include them on today's list of considerations.

Look back at Day 14 and note any of the attitudes or beliefs that contribute to depression in which you rated yourself at a level of five or higher.

Look back at Day 15 and note any spiritual issues you identified as possibly contributing to your depression by rating them at five or higher. Also note which relationship issues may be contributing to your depression and the names of the people involved.

Look back at Day 16 and note whether there is any possibility that you may be dealing with some form of repressed trauma or victimization.

ACTION

You are going to create a recovery notebook to use for preparing your personal treatment and recovery plan.

Get a three-ring binder, and add several sheets of paper.

Title the first section "Possible Contributing Factors."

In the section "Possible Contributing Factors," title each sheet with one of the possible contributing factors that apply to you. Here is the list to choose from: "Overwhelming Losses," "High Stress Level," "Chemical Imbalance," "Hormonal Imbalance," "Depression as a Secondary Symptom of Disease," "Brain Injury," "Substance in Body (Prescription or Recreational Drugs)," "Negative Attitudes," "Faulty Beliefs," "Spiritual Issues," "Relational Issues," "Repressed Trauma," and "Mystery Depression." It is not unusual if you have some contributing factors from each category discussed during the journey. If you are in doubt, include the possibility so that you can be thorough in taking care of yourself.

On each sheet titled with one of the categories of possible contributing factors, draw a line down the middle. In the left column, note the particular items that led you to believe this is a possibility or the issues you are aware of that need to be dealt with to help you feel better. Refer to your answers in previous action steps to refresh your memory. Here is an example:

Chemical Imbalance

Possible Contributing Factors	Things That Could Help
1. Moods unrelated to whether circumstances are good or bad	
2. Sleep disturbances	
3. Family history of depression (mother and both brothers suffer periodically from depression)	

SUPPORT NOTES

Today's journey takes focused concentration. To whatever degree your friend is able to do the work of putting together the notebook, let her do it. If she seems unable to focus enough to do the work, ask her questions or review the material with her as you assemble the notebook to be sure you are hearing her correctly in terms of what issues and symptoms she believes to be possible contributing influences.

ENCOURAGEMENT

You might have started out thinking there was nothing you could do to help yourself beat the blues. By defining specific possible contributing influences and issues to be dealt with, you have given yourself a measure of power. Now you have the ability to see each factor as a separate obstacle that may stand in the way between feeling miserable and enjoying life. As you choose to address each one, you will be able to knock it out of the way, either by eliminating it as a real contributing factor or by confirming that it does indeed contribute to your depression. Once you have done that, you can find the solution to deal appropriately with each remaining obstacle and find your own way to beat the blues.

Dealing with Issues Related to Normal Depression

When your bout with the blues is the normal response to an overwhelming loss or stress, you deal with it differently from other forms of depression. A slogan used by Alcoholics Anonymous is an excellent guideline when trying to get out of normal depression. It says, "The only way out is through." You may need to go through your season of grief to get over your bout with the blues in a healthy way. Here are some ideas on ways you can help yourself through this process:

Give yourself some time, but use it well. It has been said that time heals all wounds. That is true only if you use the time to treat whatever wounds you have. If you neglect a wound, whether physical, emotional, or spiritual, it may get infected and grow worse over the course of time. Use this time of pain to tend to the emotional and spiritual wounds you feel. Identify where you hurt, why you think you hurt, and get appropriate help.

Acknowledge the pain of what has happened to you. In our society pretending to be happy when you are not is seen as a virtue. We teach children to be "brave" and not cry over their hurts and losses. We admire the widow or widower who doesn't "fall apart" at the funeral. You might have learned that sorrow is not socially acceptable and adopted the habit of trying to disavow what has happened to you. You may pretend you are fine when you are not. It is important to honestly acknowledge what has happened in your life, how you feel about it, and what it means to you.

Learn to grieve. There are steps to follow in grieving a loss that will help you move beyond loss and back into a life you can enjoy. I recommend *The Grief Recovery Handbook* by John W. James and Frank Cherry. The Grief Recovery Institute can also supply referrals to qualified grief therapists or grief recovery support groups. The number to call is (213) 650-1234.

Itemize and value your losses (rather than compare them to losses of others, which tends to negate their importance). Don't minimize your losses just because they don't seem to be as severe as someone else's.

Share your pain with someone who understands. Find family members or a support group who can share the loss and sympathize with you in your time of grief.

Identify major stress factors, and take action to reduce stress as much as possible. Once you have recognized where the stress is coming from in your life, you can make choices to reduce the overall stress level.

Don't hesitate to seek counseling or inpatient treatment if you feel overwhelmed. Just because your depression comes from understandable sources does not mean that you should have to handle it on your own. If you don't feel able to manage life during this season, seek help to put your life in perspective and gain the strength to go on.

PERSONAL EVALUATION

- Do you need help in the area of grieving?
- How are you using this time of sorrow to treat your emotional and spiritual wounds?
- Are you growing better or worse with the passage of time? (If you are growing worse, you need to take action to identify and treat your wounds.)
- Are you acknowledging the reality of what has happened to you and how you honestly feel, or are you trying to pretend everything is fine?
- Do you respect the value of each loss that is important to you, or do you minimize your losses by comparing them to others'?
- With whom can you share your pain and sorrows?
- What are you doing to reduce stress in your life? What more can you do?
- Do you think you might need professional help to get you through this season?

ACTION

Go back to your notebook, and open it to the pages listing anything in the area of normal depression that may be a possible contributing factor to your bout with the blues. Look under the headings related to losses or stressors.

Discuss with your support person the things that could help you deal with the list on the left side of the sheet. On the right side of the sheet, list what you see that could help in your situation. Don't worry if you do not know where to find the resources to get the help; you will learn to do that later in the journey.

SUPPORT NOTES

There may be fear that honestly facing the pain will prove too much to bear. Encourage your loved one that you do not mind if he expresses his true feelings. Also encourage him that he will be happy again someday. If he truly seems overwhelmed, especially if he expresses suicidal thoughts, get him professional help *immediately*!

ENCOURAGEMENT

The only way out is through. As you face the reality of what has made you so depressed, you will be walking in the direction of relief. Keep moving and reaching out for the support you need to get through your valley of sorrow. You can make it through.

Dealing with Issues Related to Depressive Illness

If you have reason to believe you are dealing with depressive illness, you must get a professional evaluation. This type of depression is a medical condition that needs to be treated medically.

A chemical imbalance in the brain is caused by a depletion or deficiency of neurotransmitters (the chemicals that transmit messages between nerve endings in the brain). This condition is easily treatable using antidepressant medication, which has been widely used in recent years with much success. A physician must make the determination and administer the treatment. You may choose to receive counseling as well to help you learn to adjust to a new way of life.

If you suspect you may be dealing with a hormonal imbalance of some kind, there are things you can do to find relief. For conditions related to the menstrual cycle, women can seek treatment for PMS and other medical care to help them get through times when their estrogen-progesterone levels are fluctuating. Your doctor may suggest hormone therapy, an exercise program, or natural progesterone therapy.

If you think your depression may be related to another disease or be a side effect from some form of medication, discuss this situation with your doctor and see if there is anything medically that can allow you to treat your disease and remain free of depression.

If you are using recreational drugs that may act as depressants, you need to find a way to stop using them to free yourself from depression. You may be afraid of becoming more depressed and not being able to face life without the help of your drug. Actually, your dependence on alcohol, marijuana, or other recreational drugs may be a form of self-medication to deal with undiagnosed and untreated depressive illness. The problem is that your self-medication has temporary effects and life-damaging consequences. If you have not yet sought treatment for any addiction, consider doing so in conjunction with getting medical treatment for possible clinical depression. You may find that once the depression is treated, you will not have the same compulsive need for self-medication.

PERSONAL EVALUATION

If you still have not sought medical evaluation and treatment, what obstacles or hesitations stand in your way?

ACTION

Make an appointment and get a professional medical evaluation of your condition.

You can do this by getting a referral from your

family doctor or by contacting an inpatient treatment program in a hospital. Check to see what coverage your insurance plan offers for treatment of depressive illness.

SUPPORT NOTES

When someone may be dealing with a form of depressive illness, you cannot wait until she "feels like it" to get medical treatment. Do whatever you can to identify what is causing her to hesitate. Take whatever steps necessary to get her professional medical attention from a doctor who has a successful track record helping people with depressive illness.

ENCOURAGEMENT

If your depression has a medical cause, you will find great relief by getting medical care.

Changing Negative Attitudes and Beliefs

When you are dealing with negative attitudes and beliefs, you must change your mind to change your life. Since you have already acknowledged any negative attitudes or faulty beliefs that may contribute to your depression, you are well on your way to knowing what you need to deal with and where your mind needs to be changed. Now all you need to do is to learn how to change your mind.

You might have learned to be pessimistic. Perhaps throughout your childhood, your parents said, "Don't set your sights too high or you will be terribly disappointed." Perhaps they pointed out all the negatives, the small items you missed instead of all that you did right. If you were raised by negative or pessimistic parents, you might have learned some of the negative attitudes and faulty beliefs you previously identified.

If you learned to be pessimistic, you can also learn to be optimistic. That is precisely the point of the book *Learned Optimism*, by Martin E. P. Seligman, Ph.D. Dr. Seligman suggests you can learn to be more optimistic by developing a skill for disputing your own negative thoughts.

Research has shown that your mind will cling to foundational beliefs and throw out new ideas that disagree with your preconceived ideas, even if your beliefs are not based on truth. To change your mind, you must first acknowledge the foundational beliefs and challenge them. You start this process by accepting the possibility, however slight, that you may be wrong in your beliefs about life.

You need to take another look at your circumstances and history with the purpose of testing out a different theory. If you have previously faced life with a fatalistic attitude based on the belief that there's nothing you can do to make a lasting difference, you might have gathered evidence to prove your theory. Whenever you made the slightest effort and didn't see lasting results, you used that as proof there was no use trying in the first place.

Since you might have spent years learning to be negative, you may need to apply yourself to learning new attitudes and beliefs as well as developing the skills required to be optimistic. There is plenty of first-rate motivational material available that can teach you how to change your mind and your life. I recommend two tape series by Zig Ziglar: *Goals: How to Set Them, How to Reach Them* and *Success and the Self-Image.*

Beware of motivational materials telling you to blindly repeat positive affirmations in an attempt to improve your self-image. Telling yourself rote phrases that paint you as a picture of perfection when you are not will not help you. All that will do is add another negative belief about yourself to your list, that you are a liar!

You do need to change the way you talk to yourself but in a way that fits with reality. For example, you may catch yourself saying something negative like, "I knew today was going to be a rotten day," just because something bad happened. You can change this into a positive and realistic attitude by saying, "This is a rotten thing to happen, but I have a choice over whether I allow it to ruin my whole day."

PERSONAL EVALUATION

- Look at the negative attitudes and beliefs you have identified as possible contributing factors to your depression. Which of them are related to things you have been taught? Who taught you these things?
- Are you willing to challenge your beliefs, try out some new theories about life, and learn to be optimistic?
- Are you willing to apply yourself to developing the skills you need to replace your negative attitudes and beliefs with more positive ones?

ACTION

Go back to your notebook, and open it to the pages listing negative attitudes and faulty beliefs that may be possible contributing factors to your bout with the blues.

Discuss with your support person the things you could do to deal with the list on the left side of the sheet. Make a list on the right side of specific things that could help you change your mind to be more positive.

SUPPORT NOTES

You need to be a positive influence today. Don't focus attention on the past negative attitudes and beliefs. Instead, show enthusiasm for the possibility of learning new ways of thinking. Since the negativity was probably developed through receiving negative input, it will be important to receive positive input. Encourage using books or tapes as a way to prime the pump for positive thinking.

ENCOURAGEMENT

You really can learn things that will challenge and change your negative beliefs and attitudes. Once you begin to feed your mind on material that is positive and true, you will experience the power of a new way of thinking.

Dealing with Spiritual and Relational Issues

Spiritual and relational issues touch the heart and soul of your life. They can play a major role in developing depression. Even if these issues are not central to the cause of your depression, having a life-giving relationship with God and healthy relationships with those you love can play a key role in your recovery. This is a great time to revitalize your relationships with God and loved ones.

Spiritual Issues   Here are some suggestions for improving your spiritual life:

Cry out to God. Ask Him to receive you, guide you, and help you deal with all the issues contributing to your depression.

Confess your sins. The Bible promises, "If we confess our sins, He [God] is faithful and just to forgive us our sins and to cleanse us from all unrighteousness" (1 John 1:9). To confess simply means to agree with God about what He says is right and wrong. If you know that you have violated God's law and your own conscience, admit it. You don't have to be righteous before you do so. In fact, God says He will follow your confession with cleansing.

Express the questions and emotions you dare not say out loud. You might have cut yourself off from

God because He failed to live up to your expectations. You might have been hurt terribly or treated unjustly, and you struggle to understand how a loving God could allow such a thing to happen. You may feel tremendous anger toward God and simultaneously feel guilt or fear at the realization. God can handle your emotions and your doubts. Get them off your chest by expressing them in writing or with a spiritual counselor.

Take your spiritual questions to someone who is professionally trained to have the answers. Just as you would hesitate to treat your own physical ailments or get medical advice from someone who isn't trained in that field, don't take your spiritual questions to someone who isn't trained to understand life from a biblical perspective. Clarify your doubts and spiritual problems, then make an appointment with someone who has dedicated a life to serving God and teaching His ways.

Seek forgiveness. Being forgiven is one of the most powerful remedies for the burdened soul. Seek forgiveness from God. Acknowledge how you have hurt others, and seek to make amends, except when to do so would further hurt others.

Treat yourself to something spiritually uplifting. If it has been a while since you have been able to enjoy a spiritual experience, plan to attend a positive spiritual experience. A retreat on a positive theme, a Christian concert, or an uplifting worship service may serve to remind you that there is joy in the house of God (and that you are welcome in His presence).

Relational Issues When these issues contribute to your depression, you need to seek help that deals specifically with the kind of relational problem you are having. Try to identify the relational problems that contribute to your depression: marital difficulty, alcoholism or addiction within the family, communication problems, abusive treatment, parent-child issues, and so on. Once you have determined the central issues, you will be able to focus on finding help for you in your particular situation.

PERSONAL EVALUATION

- Even if you do not see spiritual issues as a primary cause of your depression, can you see how improving your spiritual life could help you while you work on beating the blues?
- Which of the particular items listed are you already doing?
- Are you willing to try doing some of the others? If not, why?
- What kind of relational problems relate to your depression?

ACTION

Go back to your notebook, and open it to the pages listing spiritual issues that may contribute to your bout with the blues.

Discuss with your support person the things you

could do to improve your spiritual life and renew your relationship with God. In the right column, list specific things you can do.

If there is anything you can do together immediately, do so. For example, you could pray or plan to attend an uplifting spiritual service.

Note other things you can do in the near future to improve your spiritual life.

Open your notebook to the list of names of people with whom you have relational problems. Under each name, list the primary nature of the problem. In the right column, across from each name, identify the kind of help that would most likely apply to that relational problem.

SUPPORT NOTES

These are sensitive issues. Be especially careful to keep the confidences shared regarding spiritual and relational issues. If she isn't clear on the nature of relational problems, help her identify some related issues as a starting place. If she later feels the need to seek help for relational issues, she will be able to gain a fuller picture in the process regardless of where she starts.

ENCOURAGEMENT

Improving your relationship with God and those you love can give you a source of added strength and hope.

Creating Your Personal Treatment and Recovery Plan

Recovery from a bout with the blues can constitute a major project. Just because it seems monumental does not mean that it is unreachable; you merely need to give yourself some time and rearrange your life to deal with the issues you have discovered to be contributing to your depression.

You can approach it in the familiar way most Americans purchase a home or a car. You do it on the installment plan. You calculate and negotiate the cost (what you need to do to deal with your accumulation of issues), clearly define your commitment, break the payments down into amounts you can afford, spread the payments out over a manageable span of time, and enter into a binding agreement by making a personal commitment.

When the commitment is sealed, you begin to live in the house or drive the car, even though ownership is not yet completed. It's the same with recovery. You can figure out your options, break the recovery action plan down into manageable amounts within your reach at the moment, and spread your recovery plans out over the course of moments, days, weeks, months, and years to come. You carefully consider what you need to deal with in order to live your life freely, weigh your decision, define precisely what you are committing yourself to do, then you seal the commitment with a binding agreement. You help yourself stay healthy by relying on the support system you arrange. You will continue to make payments (taking the actions you have committed yourself to, such as taking prescribed medication, reading, attending support groups, seeking treatment or counseling, making nourishing emotional choices, and so on) on a schedule as you committed yourself to do. You would also do well to have someone to whom you make yourself accountable to continue to make these payments.

PERSONAL EVALUATION

- Are you willing to rearrange your life in a way that allows you to deal with the issues contributing to your depression?
- Are you willing to set aside a block of time each week to focus on resolving the issues that contribute to your bout with the blues?
- Are you willing to make a long-term commitment to deal with the issues you have discovered during this journey, which will take time to resolve?
- Are you willing to allow someone you trust to encourage you and hold you accountable to continue making the payments necessary to live in recovery?

ACTION

Review the pages in your notebook where you have identified the possible contributing factors and things that could help.

You should have at least a few ideas to deal with each issue you have identified as possibly playing a role in your unique situation. From these ideas of things that could help, circle one or two you are willing to commit yourself to do and to continue to do over the course of time to meet your needs.

Note which ones need to be done on an ongoing basis, such as take antidepressant medication, attend support group, maintain sobriety, or continue in counseling until issues are resolved.

If you do not already have one, draw up a written schedule of how you currently spend your time. Then rearrange your commitments in such a way that you have reserved for yourself the time you need to continue making investments in your recovery and self-nurturing.

Put the specific commitment of time you are willing to make into writing along with your signature. Allow your support person to witness your commitment, and ask the person to encourage you and hold you accountable to continue living in recovery.

SUPPORT NOTES

Your long-term commitment to support your loved one will help him find the courage to make this type of life-changing commitment. Be sure to take your commitment to him as seriously as you do his own commitment to recovery.

ENCOURAGEMENT

Having a plan of action and a clearly defined commitment will lead to the goal of beating the blues and getting on with your life. Now that you know what factors most likely contribute to your depression and realize that there are things you can do to deal with the issues, you should be able to find a way to deal with whatever gets you down. Hold on to your commitments. If some of the things you try don't seem to help, adjust your plan by going back to your original list and trying other things until you find what works for you.

Finding Resources to Help You Beat the Blues

You have listed the possible factors contributing to your depression in categories. They make up the headings for the pages of your notebook. For each possible source contributing to your depression, you will need to find specific resources to deal with the issues involved.

There are several places you can look for the resources you need:

1. Yourself: personal resources of intellect, energy, determination, courage, and the like
2. Skills you can learn to help you live and think differently
3. Knowledge that will give you a new perspective
4. Individuals who will lend support to your efforts
5. Groups you can associate with to deal with issues contributing to your depression
6. Organizations designed specifically to deal with issues related to the sources of your depression
7. God, who is committed to seeing you enjoy the life He has given you

Here are the steps to finding resources in any area of interest. Since your needs are unique, you will need to follow these steps to find specific resources for you.

Step One   Identify the area where you need help or more information. (You have already done this.)

Step Two   Check at your local library for books on the topic or related topics. You can go to the card catalogue (a file of cards that represents every book available through the library). The cards are listed by topic and by author's last name. Most libraries have a wide variety of books on depression, or ask a librarian to recommend some books on the topic or guide you to the section of the library that holds the books you need.

Step Three   Contact organizations that are set up to deal with issues related to your area of interest. A great resource for any family-related issue is Focus On The Family. You can call them and receive leads about almost any conceivable family issue. The telephone number is (719) 531-3400.

- Another way to track down groups and organizations is to use your telephone directory. Look under city, county, state, and federal governments for numbers of agencies. If you are not sure that a particular agency can help you, call and explain what information or help you are trying to locate. Staff persons will usually know where to direct you if they cannot help you.
- A growing network of treatment centers and re-

covery groups has resources available. You can contact counseling offices, treatment centers, or universities and usually get leads about people, groups, and organizations that help individuals in specific ways.

- You can call the offices of radio talk shows that deal with issues related to your area of interest. Radio talk programs have to keep an extensive listing of guests who address various topics. They will probably have a list of referrals to groups and organizations as well.
- The best resources are human resources. Within your community, there are church groups, men's/women's groups, recovery groups, parenting groups, educational seminars, and so on. To tap into these meetings, you can contact your local chamber of commerce.

The real key to finding information and resources is to keep on seeking, keep on asking, and keep on knocking. Once you know what you want to accomplish, what tasks you need to complete to reach your goals, what information or help you lack, it's just a matter of persistent effort to track down the resources.

PERSONAL EVALUATION

What are three things you can do today to begin tracking down the kind of resources you need to deal with the sources of or contributing factors related to your depression?

ACTION

Do those three things! Take action today to access at least one resource. Get your hands on the resource, use the resource, or make a committed appointment to gain access to the resource within the next week. Ask your support person to help you and to hold you accountable to begin using the resources as soon as possible.

SUPPORT NOTES

Depending on the kind of action that has already been taken, your loved one may already be feeling much better. If so, allow her to move ahead on her own, and continue to encourage her. If she is not yet feeling better—as will be the case for most people dealing with grieving or normal depression—continue to do for her what she is not yet able to do for herself. Be careful not to become impatient with her.

ENCOURAGEMENT

You are not alone. There are resources to help you deal with whatever you must deal with to feel better. Keep seeking until you find the resources to help you.

Considering Using a Counselor

There are many reasons to consider using a counselor in the process of beating the blues. Here are some of them for you to consider:

Some issues that may be prime contributing factors related to your depression are hidden from your conscious mind. If you have a mystery depression, you may need the assistance of a skilled professional to help you surface and resolve repressed trauma.

Even if your depression has medical or biochemical causes, your relationships have been affected by your behavior or inability to relate well while you were depressed. These relational difficulties can often be resolved more smoothly when a counselor is involved. The counselor can help family members understand the facts of your condition and can offer advice about new ways of relating.

You might have grown used to thinking of yourself and seeing yourself in a negative haze. Counseling can guide you to ways of identifying faulty beliefs and negative attitudes and new ways of thinking in more positive terms.

If you are someone who needs antidepressant medication to deal with a depressive illness, coordinating counseling along with medical care is often recommended to monitor the effectiveness of the medication and deal with any emotional or relational problems that arise.

You might have previously sought help from a counselor who was not able to help you or who used methods that were not in keeping with your values. Just because you once went to a counselor who failed to be of help, don't discount all counselors. If you go to a counselor who does not help you, don't stop there. Keep looking until you find someone who can. You need someone you can grow to trust, someone who has a reputation of helping others and shares your values.

PERSONAL EVALUATION

- Can you see any reason counseling might be helpful in your personal recovery plan?
- What are your reasons for hesitating to seek counseling?

ACTION

Make a list of reasons that it might be helpful for you to seek counseling.

Fold a sheet of paper down the middle. On the left side, list the reasons you hesitate to seek counseling for issues related to your depression. Discuss your reservations with your support person. Then, on the right side of the paper, together list a way or ways you could move toward overcoming each reservation. For example, on the left you might write "Cost is prohibitive." On the right you could list "Check to see if insurance will pay. Find counselor using sliding fee. Call social services and churches to locate free counseling services."

Decide whether seeking counseling might be helpful to you.

Do some research to find the name of someone with a good reputation for dealing successfully with issues related to yours. Call the treatment program the person is associated with or the office to get a consultation to see if you think the counselor may be able to help you.

SUPPORT NOTES

If your loved one is willing to seek counseling at this time, do what you can to make sure the counselor has a good reputation for dealing with the appropriate issues. It can be quite discouraging to seek counseling and not find someone who inspires trust. It is acceptable to interview a therapist or counselor before beginning a counseling relationship. You may need to be involved in this process. You can call the office and ask for a preliminary consultation. Most reputable counselors will provide fifteen to thirty minutes without charge to determine if they suit your needs. Be sure to check credentials and ask for referrals.

Establishing a Support Network

The path through seasons of depression is a lonely path. You have already benefited from reaching out to your support person in the course of this journey. You also need to establish relationships with select individuals and groups who can become a support network for you.

Note that you are looking for select individuals; you are not going to return to people and groups that have contributed to your depression in an attempt to gain support from them. You are not going to try to change negative people into positive people. You are going to find people who are capable of being a support to you now.

Turn to a few friends whose involvement in your life goes beyond just helping you work through your issues related to depression. These should be relationships where you are accepted as you are, where you are free to share honestly about the struggles you are working through without having to fear rejection, and where you also learn to give of yourself to them so that the friendship is not one-sided. These people should share common interests and values.

Seek a support group whose involvement in your life is primarily focused on dealing with issues related to the sources of your depression. You may want to create a group brought together in response to your specific need, made up of individuals who are willing to make a commitment to support you as you work through these issues. This group could include others who are dealing with similar issues, others who are strong in the area of your weakness, or a mix of both. You may want to join a group already in existence that is dealing with issues related to yours.

Find a qualified counselor or therapist who has successful experience helping others work through related issues.

Consider the staff of a hospital treatment program where there is a successful track record of helping people recover from the kind of depression you are dealing with.

Discover mentors who can become positive role models as you move out of depression and toward adjusting your self-image and way of life in a more positive direction. Look for someone you admire, someone with skills, strength, and knowledge you want to acquire. You may want to seek out someone already in your circle of influence who seems to have a healthy self-regard and exemplifies positive attitudes.

Look for spiritual support persons who are willing to commit themselves to help you find and experience the love and grace of God. You could contact a member of the clergy, a lay minister, members of a group Bible study, or someone you know who seems to have a healthy relationship with God, healthy self-regard, and a willingness to walk beside you at your pace in your journey toward a closer relationship with God.

PERSONAL EVALUATION

- Who do you already know with the qualities needed to be a supportive person in your life?
- What support groups, recovery organizations, treatment centers, church groups, and so on did you discover from your previous research that might be of support to you?
- What qualified counselors and/or treatment programs in your area deal with the issues you are facing?
- Which person would you like to have as a mentor in your life?

ACTION

Complete the goal sheet for establishing your support network. Include only those you need.

Share the goal sheet with your support person, commit yourself to work on establishing a support network until the sheet is complete, and ask your support person to hold you accountable.

SUPPORT NOTES

It will take some time to fill out a healthy network of support. Your friend will need your practical help and encouragement to keep working at es-

---

Goal Sheet

The medical doctor I have consulted regarding my depression is . . .

In my support network I am seeking a few friends who will . . .

The friends I have found to fill this need are . . .

My support group is made up of . . .

The treatment/recovery program I am involved in is . . .

My therapist/counselor is . . .

The person I can call when I am in trouble and need to talk openly is . . .

My spiritual support persons are . . .

My mentors are . . .

---

tablishing a support network until it is well balanced. Don't nag. If there is hesitation on a particular point, find out what the obstacle is, and offer to be of assistance in overcoming it.

ENCOURAGEMENT

Establishing a healthy support network is a good way to avoid being overcome by depression in the future. Take care to ensure that you don't go through unnecessary pain for lack of sufficient support.

Setting Boundaries to Uphold Your Happiness

Once you have found happiness again, you can do several things to uphold your happiness. They involve the boundaries or limits you set, which protect you from falling prey to the factors that contributed to your depression. If you clearly define these boundaries now and allow the crossing of these boundaries to sound the alarm to bring your life back within the limits of what you know to be healthy for you, you will be protected from further pain.

There are some general boundaries that can help anyone stay healthy. These are some of the things you began doing at the beginning of this journey: eating a well-balanced diet, getting plenty of exercise and rest, taking a multivitamin/mineral supplement, and so on. Alcoholics Anonymous uses the acronym HALT as a reminder of some general boundaries that can lead to relapse in any kind of recovery program. The letters stand for this saying: "You should never allow yourself to become too Hungry, Angry, Lonely, or Tired." You would do well to observe these boundaries to protect against a relapse into a bout with the blues.

Everyone is more prone to depression when the stress level is too high in life. You have already noted the areas where you are prone to becoming overstressed. Set some limits to alert you of behavior that leads to stress in your life, and plan ways you can pull back and relax when life becomes too stressful.

Identify the life changes you must practice in order to deal with whatever contributed to your depression. If you need to be on medication, be careful to continue using the medication according to doctor's orders. If you find that you tend toward negative thinking, commit yourself to reading or listening to positive material on a consistent schedule.

The important thing is that you don't start to take your health and happiness for granted and stop doing the things that restored your health.

PERSONAL EVALUATION

· Where do you draw the line in terms of the basic things you do to maintain your health: body, mind, and spirit?
· What specific elements of your recovery plan will need to become a practice in order to maintain your health?

ACTION

Make a list of the limits you believe will keep you in general good health. For example, I will get eight hours of sleep each night, I will not work more than forty-five hours each week, and so on.

Make another list of the specific things related to the particular factors contributing to your depression that you need to guard as being vital to maintain your emotional health.

Share these lists with your support person, and ask for help in noticing when you are crossing the line.

SUPPORT NOTES

As time passes and the depression lifts, it is easy to grow lax in doing the things that preserve physical and emotional health. If you notice signs of fatigue or symptoms of depression, bring them up for discussion. Your loved one may become defensive, so be careful not to approach the issue with a condemning attitude. However, if she asks you to help her remain free of depression, you are allowed to lovingly present what you see happening. Ultimately, it is her choice, but she might be helped by your willingness to sound the alarm if you notice the boundaries being overstepped.

ENCOURAGEMENT

The boundaries you set now will serve to protect you in the future.

Accepting Full Responsibility for Your Life Again

While you are suffering from depression, you will be affected to some degree in ways that limit your ability to fulfill your responsibilities. Just as with any other illness, you should grant yourself some leeway while you are suffering from the condition and recovering. However, a time will come when you will be healthy enough to begin accepting full responsibility for your life. Here are some hints on when and how to do this.

While you are still suffering the symptoms of depression, you cannot be expected to function to your full potential. If you are under the care of a doctor and/or a therapist, they can help you determine the pace at which to resume your responsibilities. As you feel progressively better, you will gradually resume your responsibilities. Be careful not to demand too much of yourself too soon. Also be careful not to become reliant on your depressed mood as an excuse for failing to fulfill your roles.

There will come a time when you need to resume full responsibility for your life. Take some time to think about what those responsibilities are and who has accepted those responsibilities during your emotional and/or physical absence. The transition back into the normal flow of life can be made more smoothly if you acknowledge your appreciation for those people who have taken on your responsibilities and ask them to help you gradually ease back into accepting them.

PERSONAL EVALUATION

- What responsibilities belong to you when you are in good health that you have been limited in fulfilling while you were battling the blues?
- Which people have taken on some measure of your responsibility when you were unable to carry it?
- Are you willing to acknowledge their contribution and enlist their help as you move toward gradually accepting full responsibility for your life again?

ACTION

Make a list of the responsibilities you have neglected to some degree while you were depressed. (Note: If depression has been a lifelong problem, you might have never accepted responsibility for your life before. Now you can.)

Use these areas of life as general guidelines to spark your thinking in terms of your responsibilities: in finances, in parenting, in marriage, in the extended family, at work, in friendships, within your community, in your world, in relationship with God.

Support Notes

You will be in a position to gauge if this is something your loved one is ready to deal with now. Not everyone will be by the end of this 30-day journey, and that is OK. If your loved one is still working through issues that are deeply rooted, his season of being down and unable to assume full responsibility for life may be necessarily prolonged. If that is the case, your role is to encourage him that his health is not yet restored to the point where he needs to resume his responsibilities. If you sense he is ready, work with any counselors involved or directly with him to make the transition as smooth as possible. It will take time to get back into the habit of taking care of others.

Encouragement

As you grow healthier and happier, you will be able to resume full responsibility for your life. One day you will be better able to give to the needs of others if you make sure your needs are being met in ways that preserve your health.

Appreciating the Value of Sorrow and Pain

Even after you have beaten the blues, you cannot expect that life will ever be painless. Life in this world involves loss, death, disappointment, failure, disease, sorrow, and pain. No one is exempt. The greatest king, the lowliest beggar—all fall prey to the difficulties of life. What makes the difference is how you learn to deal with the sorrow and pain that come your way.

Sorrow and pain are not always without redeeming value. If you learn to appreciate sorrow and pain, they can have some positive effects. Here are some examples of how sorrow and pain can help you:

Sorrow and pain draw you closer to those you love. In your times of sorrow you can discover the love and compassion of those who truly care about you. You may also see false friends fall away. After your bout with the blues is over, you will have a few friends you know to be tried and true.

Sorrow and pain can act as purifying agents in life. Sometimes we experience sorrow and pain as the result of wrong behavior. They can act as a purifying fire, causing us to eliminate harmful behavior that results in pain to ourselves and others.

Sorrow and pain draw attention to areas in your body or your life that need care. Just as physical pain can lead a surgeon to the part of the body needing treatment, your emotional pain can draw attention to areas of your life where something needs to be corrected or healed.

Sorrow and pain remind us to look toward eternity. Although we will never completely escape them while we are living in these earthly bodies, they help us focus our desire on an eternal home where sorrow and pain will be relieved. The Bible promises that our eternal home is a place where God "will wipe away every tear from their eyes; there shall be no more death, nor sorrow, nor crying. There shall be no more pain" (Rev. 21:4).

PERSONAL EVALUATION

Look back over your experiences during your season of intense pain and while recovering from it. What is there of redeeming value that you can glean from these experiences?

ACTION

If you have never intellectually dealt with the problem of pain, take some time to think about the role sorrow and pain can play in your life. Discuss the subject with your support person.

If you would like some resources to spark your thinking, consider reading some of these: *A Severe Mercy* by Sheldon Vanauken, *A Grief Observed* by C. S. Lewis, *The Problem of Pain* by C. S. Lewis,

Disappointment with God by Philip Yancey, and *Where Does a Mother Go to Resign?* by Barbara Johnson.

SUPPORT NOTES

Anyone coming out of depression will need to accept that life will hold some pain. This reality may be especially frightening for those who have been overwhelmed by depression. At some point encourage discussion of what marks the difference between accepting the routine sorrow and pain life serves up and succumbing to depression. If you have not resolved these issues for yourself, it will be helpful for you to do so before discussing them with your loved one.

ENCOURAGEMENT

Once you have learned to maintain the boundaries that help you remain free from overwhelming depression, you will be better able to rebound from the sorrow and pain of everyday life.

Celebrating Your Progress

If you have persevered through each day of this journey and done your best to honestly evaluate your life and take action to improve your condition, you should be able to note significant improvements. You deserve to be applauded for exercising whatever faith you had to work with, for moving ahead when you might have felt hopeless, and for exhibiting whatever courage you could find.

Today you will evaluate and celebrate your progress. You may not be perfectly happy, but you should be able to see your way clear to know what the path to a healthier and happier future looks like. If you look carefully, you should be able to see improvement in many areas of life.

PERSONAL EVALUATION

Look back at Day 11 when you identified your assumptions and biases. Which ones were confirmed and which were adapted in the course of your journey?

Over the course of the past thirty days . . .

- How has your physical health improved?
- How has your mental attitude changed for the better?

- How has your spiritual life changed for the better?
- How has your emotional well-being improved?
- How have specific relationships within your family improved?
- How have friendships changed for the better?
- What new information did you learn that opened up new possibilities for you?
- How have your attitudes become more positive?
- How have you become more understanding of your condition?
- What have you discovered about yourself that pleased you?
- What commitments have you made that will help you live a healthier life?
- What resources are you aware of that you were not aware of before?

ACTION

Acknowledge the progress you have made and the measure of success you have attained.

Listen as your support person shares reflections on how well you did in facing these difficult issues and decisions.

Do something special together to celebrate your progress and look forward to a brighter future.

Support Notes

Prepare ahead of time to present some of your insights in terms of the progress made. Your affirmation and encouragement are very important. Go over the list of questions in the personal evaluation section, and note the specific positive changes you have witnessed. Do something special to congratulate your friend on completing her journey and to affirm your continued support.

Encouragement

Whatever measure of improvement and progress you have achieved occurred because you applied yourself faithfully to the task. You deserve to enjoy this success and to enjoy life. I wish you the very best.

Sometimes problems are too difficult to handle alone on a 30-day journey. If you feel that you need additional help, please talk with one of the counselors at New Life Treatment Centers. The call is confidential and free.

1-800-NEW-LIFE